THE COMPLETE
T'AI CHI

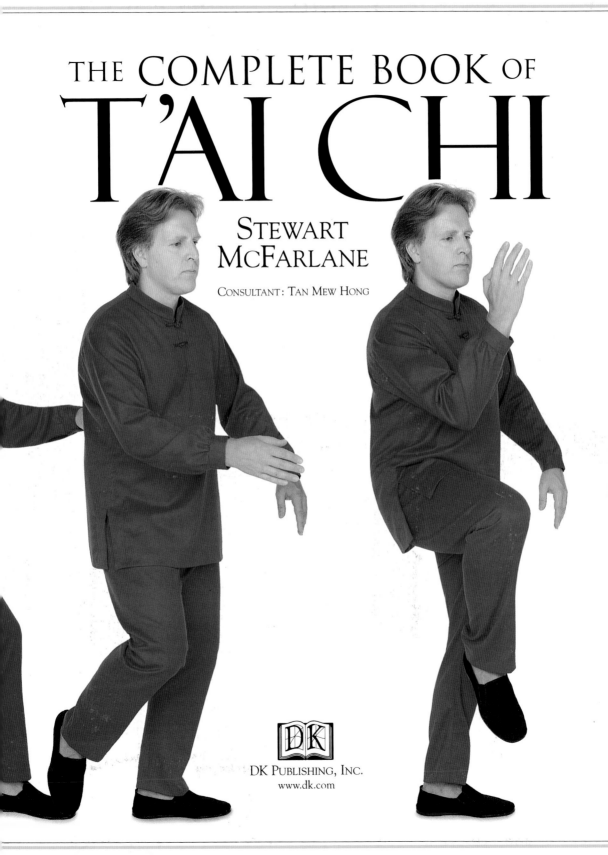

THE COMPLETE BOOK OF
T'AI CHI

STEWART McFARLANE

CONSULTANT: Tan Mew Hong

DK PUBLISHING, INC.
www.dk.com

A DK PUBLISHING BOOK
www.dk.com

Project Editor Sasha Heseltine
Project Art Editor Gurinder Purewall
Designer Elaine C. Monaghan
US Editors Laaren Brown, Leah Kennedy
Managing Editor Stephanie Jackson
Managing Art Editor Nigel Duffield
Production Controller Meryl Silbert
DTP Designer Jason Little
Senior Managing Editor Krystyna Mayer
Senior Managing Art Editor Lynne Brown

First paperback edition, 1999

First American Edition, 1997
4 6 8 10 9 7 5 3

Published in the United States by
DK Publishing, Inc.
95 Madison Avenue
New York, New York 10016

Library of Congress
Cataloging-in-Publication Data

McFarlane, Stewart.
The complete book of t'ai chi / by Stewart McFarlane
consultant, Tan Mew Hong. – 1st American ed.
p. cm.
Includes index.
ISBN 0-7894-4259-0
1. T'ai chi ch'uan. I. Tan, Mew Hong. II. Title.
GV504.M42 1996   96–33596
613.7'148 – dc20   CIP

Color reproduction by GRB, Italy.
Printed and bound in Singapore by Star Standard Industries (Pte.) Ltd.

CONTENTS

T'AI CHI SKILLS

HOW TO USE THIS BOOK

The main section of this book comprises a detailed, practical guide to the Cheng Man-ch'ing form of t'ai chi, in which a series of postures builds up into a continual sequence of movements called the form. The first section covers the health and fitness benefits associated with t'ai chi, stretching and flexibility exercises, and advice on weight distribution, breathing, and body alignment. The final section deals with the advanced t'ai chi skills of pushing hands and applications, which are performed with a partner.

THE CHENG MAN-CH'ING FORM

In this book, the moves that make up the Cheng Man-ch'ing form are broken down into individual steps to provide a detailed analysis of how each posture is achieved. General advice for the performance of each sequence is given in every introduction, and each photograph is accompanied by a caption describing the move. Additional annotations pick out specific detail, and the foot diagrams alongside each photograph show the position of each foot in comparison to the hips, giving an approximate weight distribution. Boxes holding information on testing for posture and applications are included where appropriate.

Continuation
If a sequence runs across more than two pages, this is indicated in the title of the page

Sequence title
Each sequence of the form is given its traditional name

Calligraphy
Each sequence title in the form is repeated in Chinese calligraphy

Arrow
Directional arrows indicate important changes of posture

82 MASTER CHENG'S T'AI CHI

FAIR LADY WORKS SHUTTLE

96 MASTER CHENG'S T'AI CHI

上步七星 *STEP UP TO SEVEN STARS*

At the beginning of *Step Up to Seven Stars*, the body rises from the low stance in the final stages of *Descending Single Whip* (see p. 95) by shifting the root smoothly from the right leg down through the left leg, and stepping forward with the right foot, keeping the body relaxed. It is not the root that provides a stable base from which to step forward without losing stability. The final arm stance (Step Three) can be used in application as a strong, block-and-strike combination against an opponent.

1 Rise, and shift more of your weight onto the left leg. Pivot 45 degrees to the left on the right heel, and relax the right hand, lowering it to thigh level. Raise the left arm to chest height.

2 Take a step forward and in with the right foot, placing the toes down briefly for stability. Raise the left arm to chest height, turn the wrist so that the palm faces down, and move the right arm forward.

3 Increase the weight on the left leg, and step forward with the right foot, placing the heel down first. Raise the right arm to chest height, resting the wrist just below the left wrist. Form both hands into relaxed fists.

TESTING STEP 3
To test the strength of the root down the left leg in *Seven Stars*, the instructor applies an even pressure to the student's elbows. Relaxing his shoulders, the student yields with the pressure, channeling it down through his arms, body, and left leg to the ground. At the same time, he keeps his stance firm.

PREVIOUS STAGES

Turn the Body, p. 92 — Descending Single Whip I and II, p. 93, 94

Foot diagrams
Every step of the form is accompanied by a foot diagram that shows the position of each foot in comparison with the hips.

Position of hips
Left foot is blue
90%
Right foot is red
Percentage of body weight on left foot
10% — Percentage of body weight on right foot

Previous stages
For easy reference, the previous ten steps of the form are repeated along the bottom of each left-hand page

Test box
Advice on posture testing with a partner is located in separate boxes

Introductory text
Introductions describe each sequence of the Cheng Man-ch'ing form and advise on performance

Front view
Inset photographs show the front views of stances in which the body faces away from the camera

"Master Says" box
Quotes taken from the writings of t'ai chi masters

WARD-OFF, ROLL BACK, PRESS, AND PUSH 45

RD-OFF, ROLL BACK,
ESS, AND PUSH

ence repeats a number of familiar movements, and it provides an
y to relax the hip joints and test the mobility of the waist by turning
e to side. The previous sequence (see p. 43) ended with most of the
ed in the right leg, all of which is released during *Ward-Off*, which
leg to relax. An increase in the energy stored in the body is felt
execution of the *Roll Back* section of this sequence.

張三丰
MASTER CHANG SAYS

The motion should be rooted in the feet, released through the legs, controlled by the waist, and manifested through the fingers. The feet, legs, and waist must act together.
— CHANG SAN-FENG

FAIR LADY WORKS SHUTTLES II 83

12 Turning the waist farther to the right, take a step to the right with the right foot, placing the heel down before the toes so that the heels of both feet are at an angle of almost 180 degrees to each other.

Annotation
Body movements and adjustments in weight are highlighted with detailed annotations

6 Shift most of your weight back onto the right leg to provide the momentum for the Push position (see p. 29). Move the arms, shoulders, and upper body forward into the push, bending the right knee as you do so.

Foot diagram
Every step of the Form is accompanied by a foot diagram (see box, far left)

STEP BACK TO RIDE THE TIGER 97

STEP BACK
O RIDE THE TIGER

miliar in feel to *Step Back to Repulse the Monkey* (see p. 50), this sequence offers
ther chance to step backward, gathering strength and energy, before moving
ard again. The two turns from the waist allow the body to move away from an
k, and the weight to shift from one leg to another without the feet moving.
provides the momentum for a right-handed strike in the final step, when the
of the waist to the left is coordinated with the rise of the right arm.

APPLICATION

To intercept an opponent's left-handed punch, the defender turns his waist to the right, releasing the energy in his body, and raises his arms into *Fair Lady Works Shuttles*. As he turns, the defender twists through the right leg and deflects the opponent's left arm with his right arm, leaving him wide open to a left palm strike to the chest.

Application box
Instructions on application work with a partner are located in separate boxes

"Root the weight and sink down firmly into each corner"

Quote
Additional advice is given by the author on appropriate spreads

1 Turn your waist to the right, and step to the right with the right foot, placing it at an angle of 90 degrees to the left foot. Relax both fists, and uncross the wrists.

2 Shift most of your weight onto the right leg, and turn your waist farther to the right. Lower both hands to thigh level, with the palms facing backward and the fingers relaxed.

3 With nearly all your weight on the right leg, turn your waist to the left with a strong rolling action. Raise the right hand to eye level, with the palm facing downward.

Step-by-step caption
A detailed caption describes the action shown in each photograph

---

USEFUL TERMS

The following terms are found throughout this book. Further explanations are included in the glossary (see p. 117).

Application Adaptation of the Form used in self-defense training (see p. 114).

Ch'i Internal energy flowing in channels around the body (see p. 13).

Form Series of set movements and postures that builds up into a pattern of stances that are fundamental to any martial art.

Pushing hands drills Contact drills that are performed between partners and aimed at heightening physical awareness (see p. 108).

Rooting Lowering gravity and connecting the foot to the ground by relaxing into it, to achieve balance and stability.

Sinking Relaxing and lowering the body to form a stable connection with the ground.

Splitting Taking a force coming from one direction and redirecting it to another.

Tan t'ien The area of the abdomen from which breathing is controlled during t'ai chi practice (see p. 13).

Yung ch'uan points Point on the front of the sole of each foot through which ch'i energy flows into the ground (see. p 21).

INTRODUCTION

Millions of people practice t'ai chi ch'uan every day, and it is fast becoming one of the most popular exercise systems in the world. Originating in China, it is famed for its health benefits and revered for its philosophical, cultural, and historical traditions. Disciplines similar to t'ai chi have been practiced in China for over 2,000 years, but from the 18th century onward a series of fixed postures and movements, which connect and flow into one another, evolved into t'ai chi. These set patterns of "moving meditation" are known as forms, and there are now five main and very separate styles in existence, each of differing length and method.

The t'ai chi form used in this book is the Cheng Man-Ch'ing form, brought to the West from China in the early 1960s. It is becoming increasingly popular in North America and Europe, and is considerably shorter than some of the other forms.

Anyone can practice t'ai chi; there are no physical or mental barriers to learning the form, and the best way to practice is methodically and slowly, absorbing each movement accurately, and doing at least a little work every day to build up slowly on the sequences. Although the form can be learned alone, it is useful to work with a partner on occasion, so that progress, precision of posture, and stability of posture can be monitored.

The Cheng Man-Ch'ing form can be performed easily in ten minutes, but speed is not a consideration when learning t'ai chi. It is far more important that the form be practiced at a pace that is comfortable, with the emphasis on accuracy of posture rather than speed. Learning the moves and stances of the form is just the beginning of understanding the energies and dynamics of t'ai chi; once the basics have been absorbed, advanced skills such as pushing hands and applications can be developed. These are exercises involving sustained partner work,

T'ai chi ch'uan
Citizens of Beijing practice t'ai chi in front of the Temple of Heaven.

Three Teachers
*The Buddha
(center) and sages
Lao Tzu (right)
and Confucius
represent harmony
between the three
religions of China.
T'ai chi draws on
aspects of all three.*

As an integrated exercise system for
both mind and body, t'ai chi is an
enjoyable and effective way to reduce
stress and avoid mental and physical
tension, while at the same time
helping to cultivate inner spiritual
strength and creativity.

THE ORIGINS OF T'AI CHI

Although the true origins of t'ai chi
have been lost in time and many
legends have grown around its
development, what is known is that
China has always had a strong martial
tradition. This dates back to the
feudal rivalry of the Warring States
period (402–221 BC). China was
divided into city-states, which were
defended by bands of aristocratic
warriors, some of whom were
influenced by the teachings
of Confucius (551–479 BC).
They took part in ritual
archery tournaments,
testing self-control,
poise, and resilience –
skills still important
in t'ai chi today.

Closely linked to
the history of t'ai chi is
Bodhidharma, the 6th-
century wandering
monk and founder of Zen
Buddhism. He came to
China from southern India,
and legend claims that he taught
a yoga-based exercise system to the
monks of the Shaolin temple at
Henan. This system helped to
strengthen their minds and bodies for
meditation, and it may have been
a precursor to t'ai chi in its present
form, since the regime encouraged
the mind and body to work together
to be more efficient. Shaolin temple
boxing may also have developed
from Bodhidharma's exercise system.

designed to develop acute awareness
of an opponent's actions and the
ability to anticipate their intentions.

Although nowadays often practiced
as a spiritual and physical fitness
regimen, t'ai chi was fundamentally
a fighting system, and like any other
martial art, it has its competitive side.
Practitioners attend tournaments of
pushing hands drills, and set displays
of weaponry skills – called forms – are
performed using ceremonial swords
and other traditional weapons.

WHY PRACTICE T'AI CHI?

The phrase t'ai chi ch'uan translates
from Chinese as "great polarity
boxing," drawing on the traditional
Chinese Taoist beliefs in the
interdependence of *yin* and *yang*
in the body and mind. These are
apparently opposing forces that in
fact complement each other and can
be complete only when balanced in
harmony. Skilled t'ai chi exponents
exploit the strength of the earth (*yin*)
and the energy (*ch'i*) of the heavens
(*yang*) to focus their physical and
spiritual energies so that mind and
body work together to improve
balance, stability, flexibility, and skill.

Bodhidharma
*The founder of
Zen Buddhism,
Bodhidharma was
a 6th-century
Indian monk
who developed an
exercise system that
helped improve
meditation abilities.*

CHANG SAN-FENG

The 13th-century Taoist sage Chang San-Feng is also closely connected with the mythology of t'ai chi. According to legend, he learned his martial arts at the Henan Shaolin temple and went on to train at the famous Taoist retreat at Wu-Tang. Here, as a result of a dream encounter with a warrior god, he developed a new, "soft," "internal" approach to martial arts, using the energies generated from within that are central to the practice of t'ai chi today. This was influenced by the work of Lao Tzu, the 6th-century BC founder of Taoism, which teaches that the secret of life is to live in accordance with the *Tao* ("Way"), "which does nothing, yet leaves nothing undone."

The first evidence of a familiar style of t'ai chi dates from the 18th century, with the Ch'en family of Henan province. The origins of the Ch'en family exercise system are obscure – a wandering boxer may have taught his fighting system to the Ch'en family, or it may have been developed by one of the family in the 17th century. It is impossible to say

Chang San-Feng
This 13th-century Taoist sage developed a new approach to martial arts, using internal strengths rather than brute force.

Symbol of *yin* and *yang*
The t'ai chi (or "great polarity") symbol represents the mutual dependence and harmony of yin and yang qualities. Yin is associated with darkness, softness, and water; yang with lightness, hardness, and fire.

what this early t'ai chi looked like. It may have been a series of simple exercises, with an emphasis placed on individual set positions rather than on the connecting movements.

In the 19th century the Ch'en family's exercise system was acquired by Yang Lu-Ch'an, a family servant. How Yang gained his knowledge of this system is not certain, but what is clear is that much of the recent development of t'ai chi can be attributed to him, since he established the Yang style, which is still famous today. Other styles of t'ai chi have emerged over the years, including the Wu style, a revised Ch'en style, a composite style developed by Sun Lu-Tang, and the shortened version of the Yang form, developed in the 1940s by Professor Cheng Man-Ch'ing.

PROFESSOR CHENG MAN-CH'ING

Master Cheng was born in China in 1901. He received a traditional Chinese education, specializing in painting, calligraphy, and poetry. He was a sickly child, and as a result developed an interest in health and traditional medicine. In 1932, when he was Professor of Painting at the Shanghai School of Fine Art, he began to train in t'ai chi with Yang Ch'en-Fu (1883–1936), a descendant of Yang Lu-Ch'an, in order to overcome the effects of tuberculosis. He studied with Yang for six years, learning Chinese medicine at the same time, before going on to teach t'ai chi at military academies run by the Nationalist leader Chiang Kai-Shek.

By 1946 Master Cheng had simplified the 108 positions of the Yang form into 37 moves, modifying the dynamics and skills involved, and had written his first t'ai chi book.

When the Communists took control of China in 1949, Master Cheng fled to Taiwan, establishing himself as a teacher of his new form of t'ai chi, as well as painting, poetry, and calligraphy. In 1964 he moved to New York, where he attracted a

Cheng Man-Ch'ing
Considered one of the most innovative t'ai chi masters of this century, Master Cheng Man-Ch'ing introduced t'ai chi to the West in the early 1960s.

dedicated following of students and produced a number of books on medicine, art, poetry, and t'ai chi. He died in 1975.

Master Cheng was an innovative, perceptive teacher who trained some outstanding students and inspired a generation of martial artists in Taiwan, North America, and Europe. The essence of his t'ai chi is summarized in the words "sink" and "relax." By relaxing and letting the weight sink into the legs, and lowering the center of gravity, balance is maintained and tremendous reserves of power and stability are found. Master Cheng distinguished between the strength derived from muscular contraction (*li*) and the internal strength (*ching*), which comes from correct body alignment, the opening up of joints, and relaxed muscles. This is directed to the point of least resistance with forwarding energy (*fa ching*).

T'ai chi is often called a "soft" martial art, but this does not imply weakness; instead it means yielding and not using unnecessary force to overcome an opponent.

Taoist Poet in a Landscape
This 15th-century handscroll by Chou Ch'en shows the artist dreaming of immortality in his mountain retreat. Chang San-Feng is said to have discovered t'ai chi in a dream.

T'AI CHI
BASICS

Prepare for your t'ai chi ch'uan training with a series of flexibility exercises and information on posture, body alignment, and weight distribution.

T'AI CHI FOR MIND AND BODY

The interdependence of body and mind is fundamental to traditional Chinese thought, and this is illustrated throughout t'ai chi practice, in which every move and posture is enhanced by a tranquil state of mind. The following six pages contain exercises designed to develop the initial physical skills and flexibility required in t'ai chi, and basic information on breathing, posture, body alignment, and weight distribution.

The spiritual aspects of t'ai chi are inseparable from the physical, and training develops a particular form of body awareness, which includes a sense of movement in the muscles, joints, ligaments, and bones, and an understanding of where the breathing stems from. The balance and position of the body have to be monitored constantly to increase the precision and stability of each posture, and this requires acute concentration.

SINKING AND BREATHING

T'ai chi teaches that the energy of the earth must be combined with the ch'i of the heavens (see p. 10). Master Cheng Man-Ch'ing stressed the value of being relaxed when performing t'ai chi, sinking into each posture with precision, and sinking the ch'i to the tan t'ien point just below the navel in the abdomen. The sunken, rooted feeling required in all t'ai chi practice combines with slow, deep breathing from the abdomen to produce relaxed stances that are effective in eliminating stress and tension from both the mind and body. Breathing with the diaphragm helps to lengthen and deepen the breathing, increasing the blood's oxygen supply and benefiting the internal organs. The slow turns from

the waist performed in t'ai chi are mentally and physically calming, and the slow, sunken movements of Master Cheng's form lead to inner resilience in addition to the physical benefits of stronger muscles, balance, flexibility, and a well-aligned body.

Everybody can benefit from t'ai chi
There are no physical impediments excluding people from practicing t'ai chi. The many physical and spiritual benefits can be appreciated by people of both sexes, all sizes, and all ages, including the elderly, pregnant women, and young children.

———— T'AI CHI EXERCISES ————

All t'ai chi exercises are fundamentally holistic, benefiting the whole body as well as the mind. The exercises on the following pages are especially important for specific sequences in the form, and serve to loosen and improve flexibility in different areas of the body.

EXERCISE	BENEFITS	USES IN THE FORM
Upper Body Stretch, p. 14	Establishes the weighted leg, developing rooting skills. Stretches shoulders. Aligns back and buttock muscles.	Beginning (p. 24); Single Whip (p. 31); Lift Hands (p. 32); White Crane (p. 34); Diagonal Flying (p. 54).
Waist and Hip Joint Stretch, p. 15	Mobilizes waist by loosening hip joints. Aligns and coordinates upper body, shoulders, and head.	Roll Back (p. 28); Single Whip (p. 31); Cloud Hands (p. 56); Fair Lady Works Shuttles (p. 80).
Lower Body Rotation and Stretch, p. 15	Rotates hip joints and mobilizes waist. Stretches lower back. Loosens and stretches shoulders.	Descending Single Whip (p. 60); Plant a Punch (p. 72).
Shoulder, Arm, and Hip Joint Exercise, p. 16	Coordinates arms, shoulders, upper body, and waist. Shifts root from leg to leg. Rotates hip joints.	Brush Knee, Twist Step (p. 35); Step Forward, Move, Parry, and Punch (p. 38); Fair Lady Works Shuttles (p. 80).
Rooting and Hip Rotation Exercise, p. 17	Develops rooting skills. Loosens hip joints. Coordinates arms, waist, upper body, and head.	Roll Back (p. 28); Brush Knee, Twist Step (p. 35); Step Back to Repulse the Monkey (p. 50); Cloud Hands (p. 56).

STRETCHING AND FLEXIBILITY EXERCISES

Although it is not vital to be very fit to practice t'ai chi, some degree of flexibility is required to gain the most from performing the form. The exercises shown on these pages will help you to warm up and build up flexibility. These exercises may look easy but are very effective. Hold the positions for as long as is comfortable, use gentle movements to avoid muscle damage, and take a couple of deep breaths before you start. Increase the number of repetitions slowly.

UPPER BODY STRETCH

The upper body plays an extremely important role in t'ai chi, and this exercise helps to stretch and relax the shoulders, and align the upper and lower back. It corrects the posture, so that your body is properly aligned before you begin to practice the form, and also introduces the techniques of shifting body weight from one leg to the other, and rooting through the weighted leg.

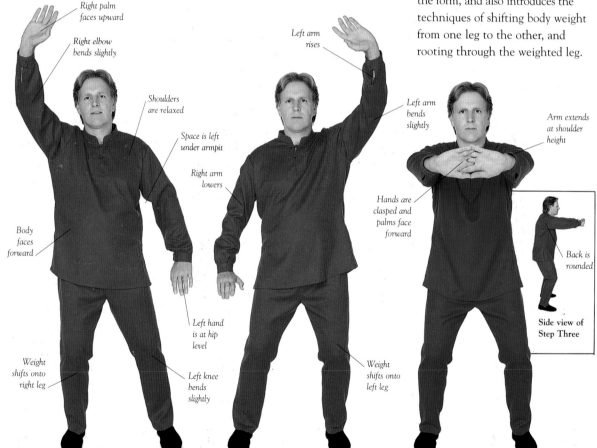

Right palm faces upward

Right elbow bends slightly

Shoulders are relaxed

Space is left under armpit

Right arm lowers

Body faces forward

Weight shifts onto right leg

Left hand is at hip level

Left knee bends slightly

Left arm rises

Left arm bends slightly

Hands are clasped and palms face forward

Weight shifts onto left leg

Arm extends at shoulder height

Back is rounded

Side view of Step Three

1 Place the feet a shoulders' width apart, and distribute your weight evenly. Keep the right elbow bent, raise the right hand above your head, and shift your weight onto the right leg.

2 Shift your weight onto the left leg, and lower the right arm until the hand is at hip level. Raise the left hand above your head, mirroring the movements in Step One.

3 With your weight evenly balanced, lower the left arm to hip level. Clasp the hands, and extend them at shoulder level. Lower the arms, unclasp the hands, and repeat the sequence.

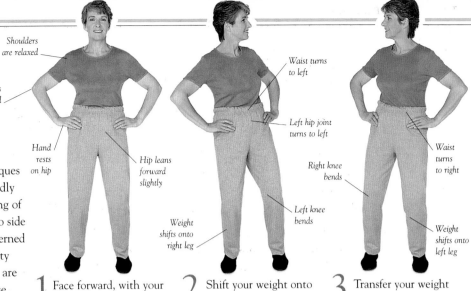

WAIST AND HIP JOINT STRETCH

One of the basic techniques of t'ai chi found repeatedly in the form is the shifting of body weight from side to side in small movements governed from the waist. Flexibility and control of the body are required to execute these moves correctly; practice repetitions of this exercise to help build up the mobility and flexibility of the waist.

Shoulders are relaxed

Elbow points outward

Hand rests on hip

Hip leans forward slightly

Weight shifts onto right leg

Waist turns to left

Left hip joint turns to left

Left knee bends

Waist turns to right

Right knee bends

Weight shifts onto left leg

1 Face forward, with your weight evenly balanced on both legs, and the feet about a shoulders' width apart. Place the hands on the hips, and breathe deeply.

2 Shift your weight onto the right leg, and turn your waist, arms, and upper body to the left, bending the left knee slightly, and making sure that your back is straight.

3 Transfer your weight onto the left leg, and turn your waist to face forward. Pause, turn to the right, mirroring Step Two, and repeat the whole exercise.

LOWER BODY ROTATION AND STRETCH

This exercise is a development of the sequence above. It is designed to aid the relaxation and rotation of the hip joints so that they turn freely. It also relaxes the waist, shoulders, and back, and develops the rounded feeling of the lower back.

Hands are clasped behind head

Shoulders are relaxed

Body bends from waist

Knee bends slightly

Waist turns to left

Upper body turns to left

Weight shifts onto left leg

Back straightens from waist

Body faces left

1 Face forward, with the feet a shoulders' width apart, and your weight evenly distributed. Relax your body and raise both arms, clasping the hands behind your head.

2 Bend forward slowly from the waist until your head is at knee level. Keep the knees slightly bent and the feet parallel. Hold for as long as you feel relaxed.

3 Shift your weight onto the left leg, and turn your waist to the left by rotating the left hip joint. Turn your upper body 90 degrees to the left.

4 Raise your upper body so that you are upright. Reverse the sequence to return to your original position, and repeat the exercise, turning to the right.

SHOULDER, ARM, AND HIP JOINT EXERCISE

This is a dynamic exercise that uses the weight of the upper body, and its momentum, to turn the waist by rotating the hip joints. The key to performing the exercise successfully is to make the arms and shoulders so relaxed that they are almost floppy. This causes the forearms to strike the chest and back at the end of each turn as they are moved from side to side. Their momentum will give a sense of the power generated when the motion of the body and limbs coordinates with the action of the waist.

Arm is raised to chest height

Shoulders are relaxed

Palm faces downward

Upper body feels weighted

1 Face forward, with the feet parallel and a shoulders' width apart and your weight distributed evenly between the legs. Raise the arms to chest height. Relax the arms and shoulders, feeling the weight of your upper body.

Left foot is parallel to right foot

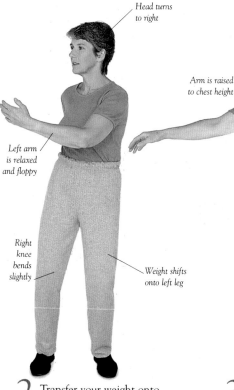

Head turns to right

Left arm is relaxed and floppy

Right knee bends slightly

Weight shifts onto left leg

2 Transfer your weight onto the left leg, and use the energy from this shift to turn your waist and upper body to the right. Swing the left arm in front of your chest and the right arm behind your back, keeping them relaxed.

Arm is raised to chest height

Body faces forward

3 Return to the original position (Step One), with the body facing forward, the arms relaxed and out to the sides, and your weight evenly distributed between the right and left legs. Pause briefly before continuing.

Head turns to left

Right arm is relaxed and floppy

Weight shifts onto right leg

Left knee bends slig[ht]

4 Transfer your weight onto the right leg, and turn your waist to the left. Swing the right arm in front of your chest, and the left arm behind your back, keeping them relaxed. Return to the original position (Step One), and repeat.

ROOTING AND HIP ROTATION EXERCISE

Building upon the benefits of the previous sequence, this exercise develops an ability to roll the waist by rotating the hip joints, and to sink weight down through the legs and feet. The latter is known as *rooting*, and provides a stable base for all movements in t'ai chi. Rooting is an invaluable basis from which to develop form (see p. 20), pushing hands (see p. 108), and application (see p. 114) skills.

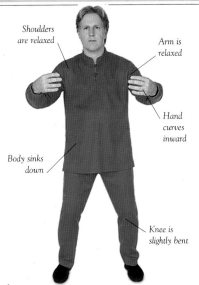

Shoulders are relaxed

Arm is relaxed

Hand curves inward

Body sinks down

Knee is slightly bent

1 With the feet a shoulders' width apart, face forward, and distribute your weight evenly on both legs. Sink the body downward, breathing with the diaphragm. Bring both arms up to form an open circle in front of the chest, leaving a space beneath each armpit.

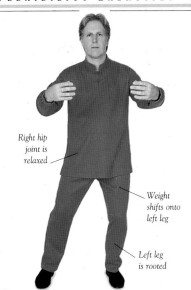

Right hip joint is relaxed

Weight shifts onto left leg

Left leg is rooted

2 Transfer your weight onto the left leg, aligning the knee over the left foot. Relax, sink your body, and root through the left leg, establishing a firm support. Let the left hip joint take the pressure of your weight, and feel the right hip joint relax.

Head turns to left with body

Arm turns to left with body

Waist turns to left

Left hip joint rotates

Left knee remains still

3 Keeping the torso relaxed, roll your upper body to the left, rotating the left hip joint. The weight of the upper body and the momentum it creates in the movement power the turn.

Left hip joint is relaxed

Head turns to right with body

Arm turns to right with body

Waist turns to right

Right hip joint rotates

Right knee remains still

Weight shifts onto right leg

Right leg is rooted

4 Still facing left, shift some of your weight onto the right leg. Relax, sink your body, and root through the right leg. With the right knee aligned over the right foot, relax the left hip joint.

5 Mirroring Step Three, roll your upper body to the right, rotating the right hip joint as you move. Repeat the whole exercise, concentrating on keeping the shoulders, arms, and upper body relaxed, and utilizing all the weight in your upper body.

PREPARING TO LEARN T'AI CHI

Three major problems affect the learning of t'ai chi, and the worst of these is tension. Although the body may feel physically and mentally relaxed, tension can creep into certain postures, particularly if they are unfamiliar, so each stance should be examined for signs of rigidity. The second fault is rushing; people should learn t'ai chi at their own pace. The third problem is lack of precision; it is vital to sink into each stance instead of flowing between movements. Each posture in the form develops specific skills, and its value is lost if one stance flows into another without the weight sinking properly. A comparison of correct and incorrect positions shows how these mistakes can affect the practice of t'ai chi.

AVOIDING TENSION

In the correct *Strum the Lute* position (see p. 36), the stance is relaxed and flexible, allowing the body weight to sink into the right leg and through the right foot into the ground. A strong connection, or "root," is formed to provide stability in the posture. The limbs bend gently, and the body is free of strain and tension. In the incorrect position (see far right), tension shows throughout the body.

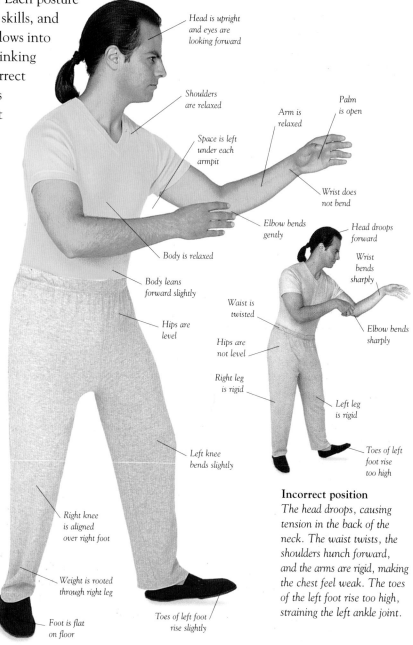

Head is upright and eyes are looking forward

Shoulders are relaxed

Arm is relaxed

Palm is open

Space is left under each armpit

Wrist does not bend

Elbow bends gently

Body is relaxed

Body leans forward slightly

Hips are level

Right knee is aligned over right foot

Weight is rooted through right leg

Foot is flat on floor

Toes of left foot rise slightly

Left knee bends slightly

Head droops forward

Wrist bends sharply

Waist is twisted

Elbow bends sharply

Hips are not level

Right leg is rigid

Left leg is rigid

Toes of left foot rise too high

Correct position
The eyes follow the direction of the arms, which are relaxed and slightly bent. The shoulders and body relax, and the lower back is rounded. The weight sinks through the right leg, the knees bend slightly, and the toes of the left foot rise slightly off the ground. The body is flexible, and ch'i flows freely.

Incorrect position
The head droops, causing tension in the back of the neck. The waist twists, the shoulders hunch forward, and the arms are rigid, making the chest feel weak. The toes of the left foot rise too high, straining the left ankle joint.

ALIGNING STANCE ACCURATELY

In the correct front view of the *Single Whip* position (see p. 31), the stance is aligned and balanced properly. The whole body is relaxed, and the limbs are flexible, bending gently but not sharply. It is important to recognize how a loose, relaxed, and balanced stance feels, and this will come only with practice and concentration. When a position feels uncomfortable (see far right), this indicates that the alignment of the whole body is wrong.

Head is upright

Right wrist is level with shoulder

Right hand forms loose hook

Space is left under each armpit

Hips are straight

Right knee is slightly bent

Fingers are relaxed

Arm is relaxed and full of energy

Waist faces forward

Left knee is aligned over left foot

Left foot is flat on floor

Right hand is floppy

Right wrist is higher than shoulder

Right arm rises too high

Waist twists to right

Hips are not level

Right knee bends sharply

Left knee falls inward

Correct position
The head is upright, the shoulders relax, and the hands are at shoulder height. The waist and the hips relax and sink, facing forward. The left knee aligns over the left foot.

Incorrect position
The right arm rises above the shoulders, and the wrist bends sharply. The left knee points inward, forcing the body to twist to the right and making the stance rigid, tense, and uncomfortable to maintain.

SINKING INTO POSTURE

The sinking of the root and weight is shown clearly in the correct side view of the *Single Whip* position. Energy flows through the arms, shoulders, upper body, and lower back into the left leg, through the *yung ch'uan* point (see p. 21) in the left foot, and into the ground. When the weight is not sunk properly (see far right), the stance becomes tense, twisted, and weak.

Head is upright

Neck is relaxed

Shoulders are relaxed

Palm is open

Wrist does not bend

Arm is relaxed

Space is left under each armpit

Body moves forward slightly

Left knee aligns over toes of left foot

Hips are level

Right knee bends slightly

Right leg extends slightly

Weight is on left leg

Right foot is flat on floor

Weight is rooted through left foot

Neck is tense

Shoulders are stiff

Body hunches forward

Waist is twisted

Wrist bends

Arm is tense

Hips are not level

Right knee does not bend

Left knee bends out to left

Correct position
The body relaxes, the weight is evenly balanced, and the left knee aligns over the left foot. The weight sinks down through the left hip into the left leg and down through the foot. The arms are slightly bent and can move freely.

Incorrect position
The body is rigid, the limbs are stiff, and the waist twists. This impedes the flow of ch'i energy and reduces the ability of the limbs to store the energy so that they cannot move easily.

MASTER CHENG'S
T'AI CHI

Begin your practice of t'ai chi ch'uan by running
through a preparation checklist, and move
on to learning Master Cheng's form.

T'AI CHI PREPARATION

It is essential to be in a mental and physical state of relaxed awareness before practicing the form. Stand quietly in a peaceful environment, and take a few deep breaths. Deepen your breathing, filling the lower half of your lungs first, and allow your diaphragm to stretch down toward the *tan t'ien* (see p. 13) in the abdomen. Work in numerical order through the points shown below, and move onto the form.

Side view of
***Preparation* stance**

Chin is tucked in to align head and upper body

Lower back is rounded

Knees align with end of toes

Front view of
***Preparation* stance**

1. *Head is held as if suspended by a thread from crown*

2. *Eyes look ahead but are slightly lowered; peripheral vision is used*

3. *Facial muscles are relaxed*

4. *Mouth is relaxed – neither wide open nor tightly closed*

5. *Tip of tongue is placed on roof of mouth*

6. *Shoulders are relaxed and rounded*

7. *Back is slightly rounded, and chest is hollowed*

8. *Space is left under each armpit*

9. *Elbow joints are relaxed and rounded*

10. *Fingers of both hands are relaxed – neither straight nor bent*

11. *Space is left between thumb and index finger of each hand*

12. *Hips are relaxed; hip joints feel as if they are hanging loose*

13. *Backside is tucked in, buttock muscles and thighs are relaxed*

14. *Knees are slightly bent, and calves and thighs are free of tension*

15. *Feet are relaxed and rest flat on ground*

16. *Weight falls through yung ch'uan points on soles of both feet (see right)*

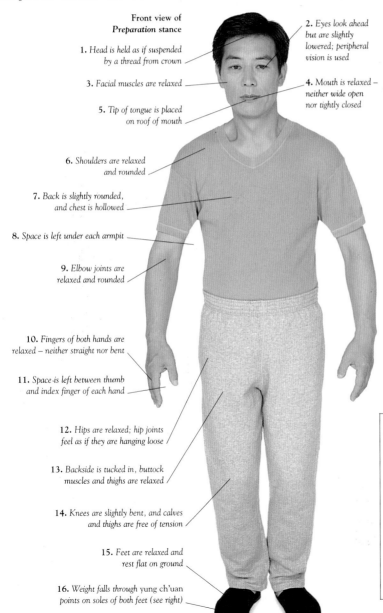

The preparation stance

When preparing for the form, relax your body, bend both knees, and rest the hands at thigh level. The upper body feels light, and the lower body heavy, with the weight rooted through the yung ch'uan points (see below). Tuck in the chin to align the head and upper spine, opening the energy channels in your body, allowing the ch'i (see p. 11) to flow.

— YUNG CH'UAN POINTS —

The *yung ch'uan* points are on the front of the soles of both feet. From these points, *ch'i* forms a physical connection, or "root," with the ground. T'ai chi facilitates the flow of *ch'i* through the energy channels of the body.

Left yung ch'uan point

Yung ch'uan point is in center of ball of foot

預備式 PREPARATION

There is some discussion among practitioners as to whether these first, small, actions are part of Cheng Man-ch'ing's original form, but they are always included in its performance. They introduce techniques used throughout the form, such as the shifting of weight from one leg to the other, the sinking of the weight, and the moving of the waist from side to side. To relax the mind and body, the t'ai chi checklist (see p. 21) is always worked through before the form is practiced. Before starting *Preparation*, the weight is pushed through the *yung ch'uan* point, and three slow, deep, breaths are taken from the *tan t'ien* (see p. 21), helping to create a calm state of mind.

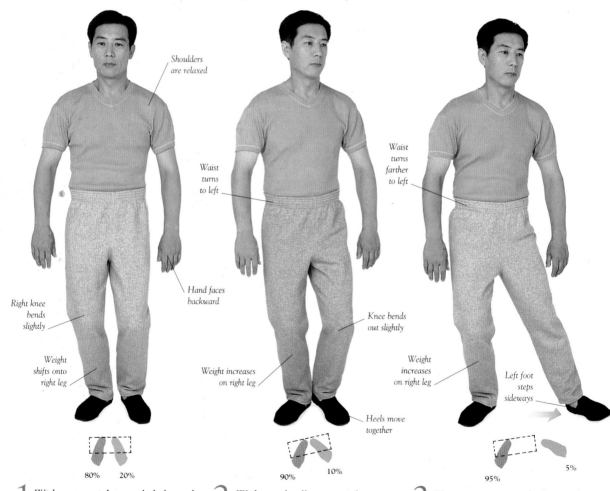

Shoulders are relaxed

Waist turns to left

Waist turns farther to left

Hand faces backward

Knee bends out slightly

Right knee bends slightly

Weight shifts onto right leg

Weight increases on right leg

Weight increases on right leg

Left foot steps sideways

Heels move together

80%   20%

90%   10%

95%   5%

1 With your weight evenly balanced, stand upright and face forward, relaxing the shoulders and hips. Allow the arms to hang by your sides. Shift most of your weight onto the right leg, bending the right knee slightly.

2 With nearly all your weight on the right foot, turn your waist slightly to the left, moving both arms around with your body. As you move, bring the heels together, bending both knees sideways to relax the hip joints.

3 Turning your waist farther to the left, take a step to the left with the left foot about a shoulders' width from the right foot. Place the left heel down on the ground first, and put a small amount of your weight onto it.

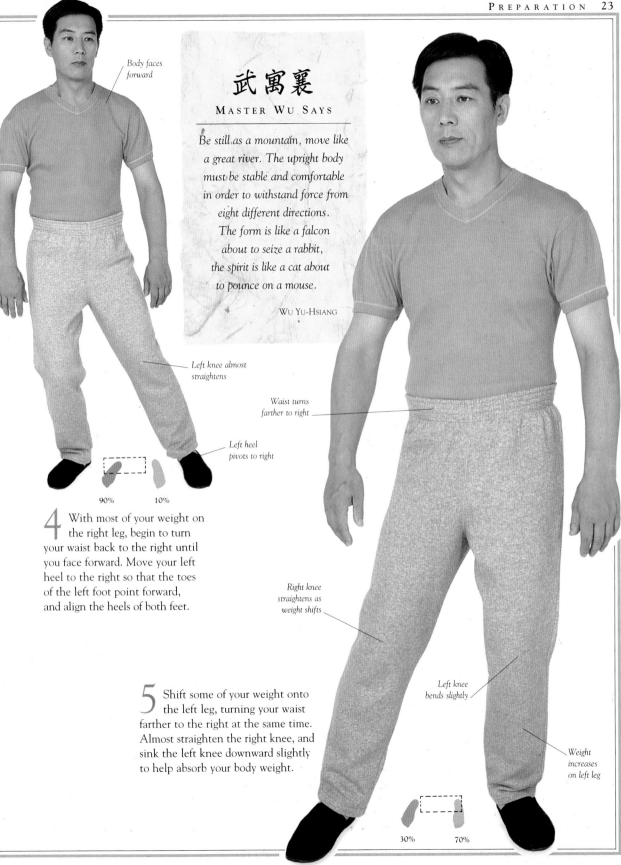

Body faces forward

武寓襄

MASTER WU SAYS

Be still as a mountain, move like a great river. The upright body must be stable and comfortable in order to withstand force from eight different directions. The form is like a falcon about to seize a rabbit, the spirit is like a cat about to pounce on a mouse.

WU YU-HSIANG

Left knee almost straightens

Waist turns farther to right

Left heel pivots to right

90%   10%

4 With most of your weight on the right leg, begin to turn your waist back to the right until you face forward. Move your left heel to the right so that the toes of the left foot point forward, and align the heels of both feet.

Right knee straightens as weight shifts

Left knee bends slightly

5 Shift some of your weight onto the left leg, turning your waist farther to the right at the same time. Almost straighten the right knee, and sink the left knee downward slightly to help absorb your body weight.

Weight increases on left leg

30%   70%

起勢 BEGINNING

The opening sequence of the Cheng Man-ch'ing form focuses on the controlled, slow movement of the arms, while keeping the body weight evenly balanced. It is important to be relaxed enough to feel the weight of the arms as they move up and down. The key to this is to relax the muscles in the forearms, which will give them a heavy, weighted feeling, and avoid using the muscles in the shoulders. This feeling should be applied throughout the form, and helps when learning t'ai chi applications, since the limbs and hands need to be relaxed to respond to another person's movements.

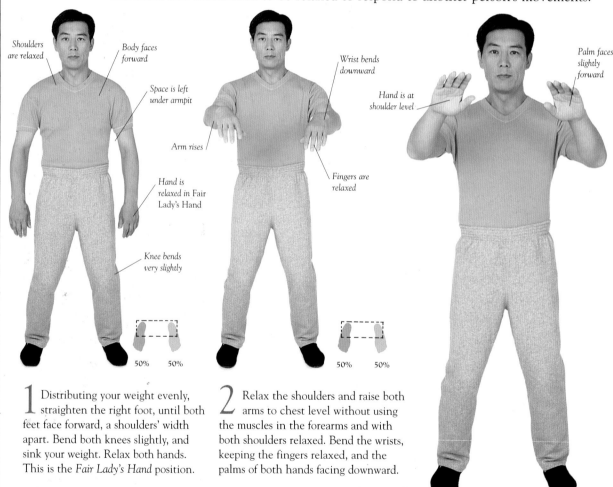

Shoulders are relaxed · *Body faces forward* · *Space is left under armpit* · *Arm rises* · *Hand is relaxed in Fair Lady's Hand* · *Knee bends very slightly*

Wrist bends downward · *Hand is at shoulder level* · *Fingers are relaxed*

Palm faces slightly forward

50% 50%   50% 50%

1 Distributing your weight evenly, straighten the right foot, until both feet face forward, a shoulders' width apart. Bend both knees slightly, and sink your weight. Relax both hands. This is the *Fair Lady's Hand* position.

2 Relax the shoulders and raise both arms to chest level without using the muscles in the forearms and with both shoulders relaxed. Bend the wrists, keeping the fingers relaxed, and the palms of both hands facing downward.

3 Raise the forearms until both hands are at shoulder level, with the palms facing slightly forward and the fingers extended upward.

50% 50%

PREVIOUS STAGE

Preparation, p. 22

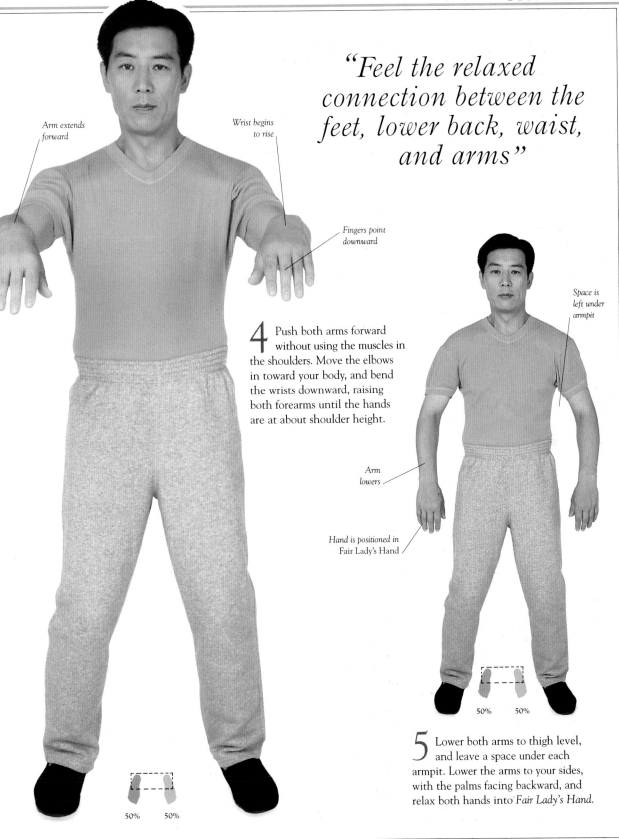

Arm extends
forward

Wrist begins
to rise

*"Feel the relaxed
connection between the
feet, lower back, waist,
and arms"*

Fingers point
downward

4 Push both arms forward
without using the muscles in
the shoulders. Move the elbows
in toward your body, and bend
the wrists downward, raising
both forearms until the hands
are at about shoulder height.

Space is
left under
armpit

Arm
lowers

Hand is positioned in
Fair Lady's Hand

50%   50%

50%   50%

5 Lower both arms to thigh level,
and leave a space under each
armpit. Lower the arms to your sides,
with the palms facing backward, and
relax both hands into *Fair Lady's Hand*.

左掤 LEFT WARD-OFF

When *Left Ward-Off* is combined with *Right Ward-Off* (see p. 27) and *Roll Back, Press, and Push* (see p. 28), they form an extended sequence known as *Grasp the Sparrow's Tail*. Step One of *Left Ward-Off* introduces an arm position that is repeated many times throughout the form; the hands are placed in front of the body as if holding an imaginary ball above either thigh, one hand appearing to support the imaginary ball from below and the other appearing to rest on top of the ball.

1 Turn your waist to the right, and shift your weight onto the left leg. Pivot on the right foot to the right, placing the hands as if holding an imaginary ball above the right thigh, the right hand on top.

Right foot is at right angle to left foot

Weight is on left leg

10%

90%

2 Shift nearly all your weight forward onto the right leg, and feel the energy flowing in both legs as you transfer your weight. Straighten your upper body, keeping the back muscles relaxed.

Weight shifts onto right leg

90%

10%

Left leg extends

Left arm is in Ward-Off position

Waist turns to left

Right knee bends

Weight increases on left leg

Right foot pivots to left on heel

30%

70%

3 Take a small step forward with the left foot, leaving about one shoulders' width between the feet. Place the left heel down first, before rolling the rest of the foot down.

Left leg moves forward

90%

10%

4 Shift your weight onto the left leg, and turn your waist toward the left. Raise the left forearm to chest level, with the palm facing inward, and lower the right arm. Leave a space under each armpit.

Left forearm rises to chest height

Weight shifts onto left leg

40%

60%

5 Turn your waist to the left, and pivot the right foot to the left on the heel. At the same time, raise the left arm in front of your chest, forming the *Left Ward-Off* position, and lower the right arm.

PREVIOUS STAGES

— Preparation, p. 22 —   — Beginning, p. 24 —

右 掤 RIGHT WARD-OFF

This sequence follows on from *Left Ward-Off* here and twice more in the form. There are several important differences between the final postures of the two sequences. In *Left Ward-Off* the left hand crosses the body, and the right hand is placed by the thigh, while in *Right Ward-Off* the right arm extends upward, and the left arm is placed below. With practice, it is possible to move from one *Ward-Off* position to the other with a single shift of weight and a small turn of the waist.

1 Increasing the weight on the left leg, sink it down, and turn your waist slightly to the left. Mirroring Step One (opposite), place the hands as if holding an imaginary ball above the left thigh, with the left hand resting on top and the right hand below.

Waist turns to left

Weight increases on left leg

Right arm is in Right Ward-Off position

Shoulders are relaxed

Left arm is slightly lower than right

Stomach muscles are relaxed

Waist turns farther to right

Left leg extends

Right knee bends

Left arm crosses chest

Right arm lowers

Waist turns to right

Weight shifts onto right leg

20%

80%

70%

30%

2 Placing a little more weight on the left leg, turn your waist to the right, step forward and slightly to the right with the right foot, and place the heel down first. As you move, lower the right arm to thigh level, and move the left arm across your chest.

15%

Right foot steps to right

85%

3 Shift most of your weight onto the right leg, and turn your waist farther to the right. Twist the left foot to an angle of 45 degrees behind the right foot, and move the right hand to shoulder height, forming the *Right Ward-Off* position.

攦擠按 ROLL BACK, PRESS, AND PUSH

The three stages of this sequence are powered from the waist, while the upper body remains still. In *Roll Back*, the hip joints are relaxed to allow the waist to move without restriction. It is important that the stance is precise at each stage of the sequence to give stability. While performing *Press* and *Push*, there should be a feeling of energy flowing from the base of the spine into the foot. This is vital in developing *fa ching*, the springing energy that provides much of the momentum for moving forward.

1 Shift nearly all your weight onto the right leg, and turn your waist farther to the right. Relaxing the right hip joint, twist the right wrist counterclockwise slightly, relieving the tension in the forearm.

Right wrist rotates

Waist turns slightly to right

Right arm bends inward

Waist turns farther to left

Left forearm lowers

Hand is loosely rounded

85%

15%

Weight increases on right leg

Weight increases on left leg

2 Transfer most of your weight onto the left leg, turning your waist to the left. Move your upper body and arms to the left as you turn your waist.

Waist turns to left

Weight shifts onto left leg

20%

80%

15%

85%

3 Increasing the weight on the left leg, turn your waist farther to the left. As your body turns, lower the left forearm, with the hand loosely rounded, and bend the right arm in and slightly across your body at chest height, with the palm facing inward. This is the *Roll Back* position.

PREVIOUS STAGES

Beginning, p. 25   Left Ward-Off, p. 26   Right Ward-Off, p. 27

4 Shift your weight onto the right leg, and turn your waist to the right. Bring the left arm upward in a sweeping movement across your body until the hand is positioned just behind the right arm. As your waist moves, turn the right palm to face the left hand.

Right arm is in front of left hand

Left arm rises

Weight shifts onto right leg

60%

40%

5 Transferring more of your weight onto the right leg, cradle the left hand in the right hand so that the palms face each other. The hands are now in the *Press* position. Move your upper body slightly forward, using the lower back muscles.

Right hand supports left hand

Upper body moves forward

Hands are in Press position

Left leg extends backward

Weight increases on right leg

85%

15%

Fingers extend upward slightly

Weight shifts onto left leg

20%

80%

6 Moving the hands slightly apart just below shoulder height, shift nearly all your weight onto the left leg. Keep the fingers of both hands gently curved, with the palms facing downward.

Arms extend in Push position

Upper body pushes forward from waist

Front view of Push position

Hands extend at chest height

7 Shift nearly all your weight forward onto the right leg, pushing the body slightly forward and bending the leg to absorb your body weight. Push your body forward and upward, with the arms extending upward and both palms facing down. This is the *Push* position.

95%

5%

TURN THE BODY, AND LOWER THE HANDS

轉身掉手

Repeated three times in the form, *Turn the Body, and Lower the Hands* may have been added to Master Cheng's original form to facilitate a difficult change of posture from the *Push* stance (see p. 29) to the various *Single Whip* sequences. Its purpose is to shift the weight subtly from one direction to the other, release tension built up in the *Push* position, work the arms, waist, and body together, and produce the energy to power *Single Whip*.

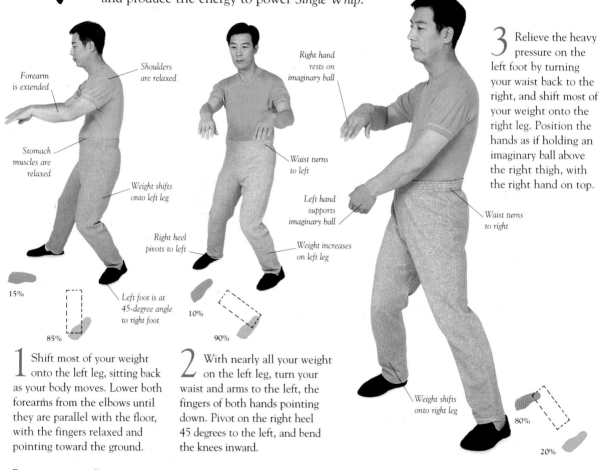

Forearm is extended

Shoulders are relaxed

Stomach muscles are relaxed

Weight shifts onto left leg

Right heel pivots to left

Left foot is at 45-degree angle to right foot

15%

85%

Right hand rests on imaginary ball

Waist turns to left

Left hand supports imaginary ball

Weight increases on left leg

10%

90%

3 Relieve the heavy pressure on the left foot by turning your waist back to the right, and shift most of your weight onto the right leg. Position the hands as if holding an imaginary ball above the right thigh, with the right hand on top.

Waist turns to right

Weight shifts onto right leg

80%

20%

1 Shift most of your weight onto the left leg, sitting back as your body moves. Lower both forearms from the elbows until they are parallel with the floor, with the fingers relaxed and pointing toward the ground.

2 With nearly all your weight on the left leg, turn your waist and arms to the left, the fingers of both hands pointing down. Pivot on the right heel 45 degrees to the left, and bend the knees inward.

PREVIOUS STAGES

Right Ward-Off, p. 27 ——— Roll Back, Press, and Push, p. 28

單鞭 SINGLE WHIP

With variations and additions, *Single Whip* is performed five times in the form, and with the subtle shifting of the body position and rooted footwork leading up to the final position, this sequence uses up much of the energy stored during the preceding moves. In application, the loose hook shape formed by the right hand can be used to push an opponent away. In Step Four, all the limbs are extended, and the shoulders, elbows, and wrists must be relaxed. In the words of the *T'ai chi Classics* (see p. 9), the limbs should be "straight, but not straight; bent, but not bent".

Right hand forms loose hook

Waist turns to left

90%

Left foot pivots to left

10%

1 Start to turn your waist to the left, moving both arms with your body, forming a loose hook with the right hand. Increase the weight on the right leg, raise the left heel, and pivot to the left on the ball of the foot.

Waist turns farther to left

Left foot steps backward

10%

90%

2 With nearly all your weight still on the right leg, step backward with the left foot to a shoulders' width from the right foot. Turn your waist farther to the left, moving the arms as you do so.

Fingers of left hand point forward

4 Continue to turn your waist to the left, increasing the weight on the right leg. Raise the left forearm, extend it forward at shoulder height, and point the fingers forward.

Weight decreases on left leg

3 Turn your waist to the left, and shift most of your weight onto the left leg. Pivot 90 degrees to the left on the right heel, raising the left hand to shoulder level.

Waist turns to left

Left arm rises

Weight shifts onto left leg

80%

20%

70%

30%

Front view of Single Whip

Right arm extends at shoulder height

提手 LIFT HANDS

Although it appears to be a small move, *Lift Hands* gives the expansive feeling of gathering up two types of energy. With practice, both arms will begin to feel as if they are scooping up *chi* (see p. 21) into a round space in front of the chest. Secondly, the shift in weight from the right leg to the left leg will give the effect of storing up springing energy from the ground. This will facilitate fast, fluent movement from one leg to the other. Master Cheng recommended regular practice of this posture to develop leg muscles and rooting skills.

Right forearm lowers

Shoulders are relaxed

Right hand rises

Left hand is loosely rounded

Right hip is relaxed

2 With nearly all your weight on the left leg, relax the right hip, and move the right leg slightly to the left, raising the toes slightly. Extend and raise the right arm. Relax your shoulders and hips, and leave a space under each armpit.

Waist turns to right

1 With most of your weight on the left leg, turn your waist to the right. Pivot 45 degrees to the right on the right heel, lower both arms slightly, and curve the hands inward.

Weight increases on left leg

Toes of right foot are slightly raised

90%

10%

80%

20%

— TESTING STEP 2 —

To test the stability of *Lift Hands*, the student sinks into position, rooting through his left leg, while the instructor applies gentle pressure to his upper arms. As the student relaxes his shoulders and channels the instructor's energy down through the arms, shoulders, body, and left leg into the ground, his stance should not falter.

Even pressure is applied to upper arm

Weight is rooted through left leg

Student

Instructor

PREVIOUS STAGES

Roll Back, Press, and Push, p. 28 ⌐ ⌐ Turn the Body, p. 30 ⌐ ⌐ Single Whip, p. 31

靠 SHOULDER STRIKE

In *Shoulder Strike*, some of the forwarding energy (*fa ching*) stored in *Lift Hands* is released when the weight shifts from one leg to the other (Step Three). This eliminates tension created in the leg during earlier movements. The sequence is useful both as a close-range fighting application, since it contains a shoulder strike in Step Two, and at a longer range, using the elbow strike in Step Four as an opponent retreats.

1 Draw the right heel in toward the left heel, and rest the right foot there with the heel slightly raised. Bend both knees, and let them fall open slightly. Lower both arms so that the left hand rests across the stomach, and the right hand rests in front of the right thigh.

Left arm crosses body

Right arm lowers

Right hand rests in front of right thigh

Right foot moves to left

90%

10%

2 Turn your waist to the right, and step forward with the right foot. Place the heel down first, and turn the left foot slightly to the right.

Shoulder is in Strike position

Waist turns to right

Elbow is in Strike position

Left knee sinks

Left foot turns to right

Right foot steps forward

90%

10%

3 Shift most of your weight onto the right leg, and turn your waist farther to the right. Move the right elbow forward, and rest the left hand close by the right elbow.

Waist turns to right

Right knee bends

Weight shifts onto right leg

40%

60%

Waist moves to right

Weight increases on right leg

30%

70%

4 Increase the weight on the right leg, sinking downward onto the leg. Continue turning your waist and arms to the right.

白鶴亮翅 WHITE CRANE SPREADS ITS WINGS

In Chinese tradition, cranes have long been regarded as symbols of longevity and resilience as well as beauty and fragility, and this sequence shows how such apparently opposing *yin* and *yang* forces can work together in perfect balance and harmony. For instance, the arms and legs move in opposite pairs: the left leg and right arm feel light and full of energy, while the firm root down through the right leg combines with the weighted sensation in the left arm.

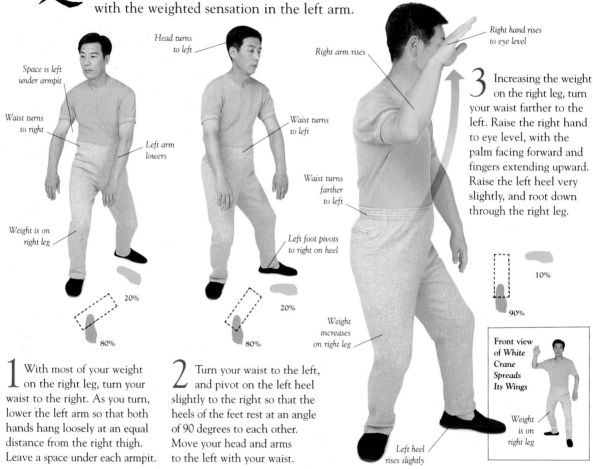

Space is left under armpit

Head turns to left

Waist turns to right

Left arm lowers

Weight is on right leg

20%

80%

Waist turns to left

Waist turns farther to left

Left foot pivots to right on heel

20%

80%

Right arm rises

Right hand rises to eye level

Weight increases on right leg

Left heel rises slightly

10%

90%

1 With most of your weight on the right leg, turn your waist to the right. As you turn, lower the left arm so that both hands hang loosely at an equal distance from the right thigh. Leave a space under each armpit.

2 Turn your waist to the left, and pivot on the left heel slightly to the right so that the heels of the feet rest at an angle of 90 degrees to each other. Move your head and arms to the left with your waist.

3 Increasing the weight on the right leg, turn your waist farther to the left. Raise the right hand to eye level, with the palm facing forward and fingers extending upward. Raise the left heel very slightly, and root down through the right leg.

Front view of **White Crane Spreads Its Wings**

Weight is on right leg

PREVIOUS STAGES

Single Whip, p. 31 — Lift Hands, p. 32 — Shoulder Strike, p. 33

BRUSH KNEE, TWIST STEP

摟
膝
拗
步

The first of two repetitions of this movement in the form is broken up by *Strum the Lute* (see p. 36). The power in *Brush Knee, Twist Step* comes from the rolling action of the waist as it moves from side to side, which provides the momentum for the relaxed, but still carefully controlled, movement of both arms. As in the previous sequence, the arms and legs work together in opposing pairs, and their movement should be smoothly coordinated, with a strong feeling of energy flowing between the right hand and the *yung ch'uan* point (see p. 21) in the left foot, and vice versa.

1 Continue to turn your waist to the left, and lower the right arm to thigh level, with the fingers of the right hand pointing downward.

Right arm lowers

Fingers of right hand point downward

Waist turns farther to left

10%

90%

Right hand rises

2 Transfer a little more weight on to the left leg, and turn your waist to the right until your body is facing forward. Relax both arms at thigh level, which is the *Bear* position, and move the arms to the right with your body.

...m is Bear ...ition

Waist turns) right

Weight increases slightly on left leg

20%

80%

Weight increases on right leg

Left heel is placed down first

10%

90%

3 Increasing the weight on your right leg, step to the left with the left foot, keeping it at an angle of 90 degrees to the right foot, and placing the heel down first. Start to raise the right arm, brushing the left palm past the left knee.

Left leg steps out to left

4 Shift your weight onto the left leg, turn your waist to the left slightly, and sink forward. Raise the right forearm so that the hand is level with the right ear.

Right arm rises

Waist turns to right

Weight shifts onto left leg

60%

40%

Waist turns to left

5 Turning your waist to the left, shift most of your weight onto your left leg. As you turn, pivot 45 degrees to the left on the right heel, and lower the right arm.

Right foot pivots to left on heel

70%

30%

STRUM THE LUTE

手揮琵琶

The name of this sequence is significant in that it emphasises the essentially nonaggressive nature of t'ai chi, and is appropriate since the hand movements of the final position are reminiscent of a musician strumming on the strings of a lute. In its overall feeling, it is similar to *Lift Hands* (see p. 32), requiring the development of strong rooting skills. The main difference between the two sequences is that the weight is rooted through opposite legs; here the weight is rooted firmly down through the right leg, and the left arm and leg move forwards together.

1 Increase the weight on the left leg, and turn your waist slightly toward the right. Take a small step forward with the right foot, placing it on the ground at an angle of about 90 degrees to the left foot.

Waist turns to right

Weight increases on left leg

Right foot steps forward

Waist turns to left

90%

10%

Stomach muscles are relaxed

Weight shifts onto right leg

Right hand begins to lower

Left hand begins to rise

2 Shift most of your weight onto the right leg, and turn your waist slightly to the left. Begin to raise the left hand and lower the right hand until they are both at chest height.

20%

80%

Body bends slightly forward

Left arm rises to chest height

3 With nearly all your weight on the right leg, take a step forward and to the right on the left foot, placing the heel down first. Rest both arms briefly at about chest height, and feel the energy in both hands.

Weight increases on right leg

Left foot steps forward and right

Left heel is placed down first

90%

10%

PREVIOUS STAGES

├─ p. 33 ─┤ ├─ White Crane, p. 34 ─┤ ├─ Brush Knee, Twist Step, p. 35 ─┤

BRUSH KNEE, TWIST STEP

撂
膝
拗
步

This is a repetition of the previous *Brush Knee, Twist Step* (see p. 35), and again shows the importance of the legs and arms working together in diagonal pairs. As the left leg bends in the final stance, the right arm is brought forward, and *chi* energy flows between them. By coordinating the movements of the right arm with the leg, and vice versa, a total balance and harmony of movement can be achieved as the sequence is performed. The power generated by turning the waist to the left helps both arms feel weighted, adding strength to their relaxed but controlled movements.

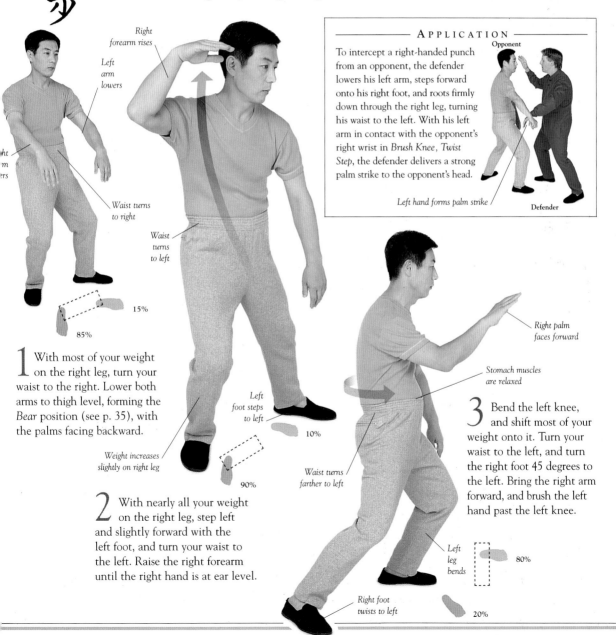

Right
forearm rises

Left
arm
lowers

Waist turns
to right

Waist
turns
to left

15%

85%

1 With most of your weight on the right leg, turn your waist to the right. Lower both arms to thigh level, forming the *Bear* position (see p. 35), with the palms facing backward.

Weight increases
slightly on right leg

Left
foot steps
to left

10%

90%

Waist turns
farther to left

2 With nearly all your weight on the right leg, step left and slightly forward with the left foot, and turn your waist to the left. Raise the right forearm until the right hand is at ear level.

APPLICATION

Opponent

To intercept a right-handed punch from an opponent, the defender lowers his left arm, steps forward onto his right foot, and roots firmly down through the right leg, turning his waist to the left. With his left arm in contact with the opponent's right wrist in *Brush Knee, Twist Step*, the defender delivers a strong palm strike to the opponent's head.

Left hand forms palm strike

Defender

Right palm
faces forward

Stomach muscles
are relaxed

3 Bend the left knee, and shift most of your weight onto it. Turn your waist to the left, and turn the right foot 45 degrees to the left. Bring the right arm forward, and brush the left hand past the left knee.

Left
leg
bends

80%

Right foot
twists to left

20%

進步搬攔捶 STEP FORWARD, MOVE, PARRY, AND PUNCH

The strength in this sequence comes from the movement of the entire body, with the power emanating from the rolling action of the waist. With practice, your arms will feel relaxed and should follow the movement of the waist as it turns from side to side. When broken down into its four component parts, the sequence's potential for self-defense can be easily seen; the *Parry* and *Punch* stances combine with the swinging waist movements to deflect and unbalance an opponent.

1 Turn your waist to the left, and sit back onto the right leg. Straighten the left leg, and pivot 45 degrees to the left on the left heel, raising the toes slightly. Lower the right arm to thigh level, and form a loose fist with the right hand.

Waist turns to left

Right hand forms loose fist

Weight is on right leg

Left leg straightens

Toes of left foot are raised

Left heel pivots to left

20%

80%

2 Shift most of your weight onto the left leg, and place the left foot flat onto the floor, bending the left knee as you do so. At the same time, begin to turn your waist back to the right.

Waist turns to right

Weight shifts onto left leg

80%

20%

3 With more weight on the left leg, trace an arc with the right heel toward the left foot, bringing the foot to rest at an angle of 90 degrees to the left foot and about a shoulders' width away. Simultaneously, trace the path of the right foot with the right fist, and raise the left arm.

Left arm rises

Right fist moves in arc to left

Right heel moves forward

90%

10%

PREVIOUS STAGES

Brush Knee, Twist Step, p. 35 — Strum the Lute, p. 36 — Brush Knee, Twist Step, p. 37

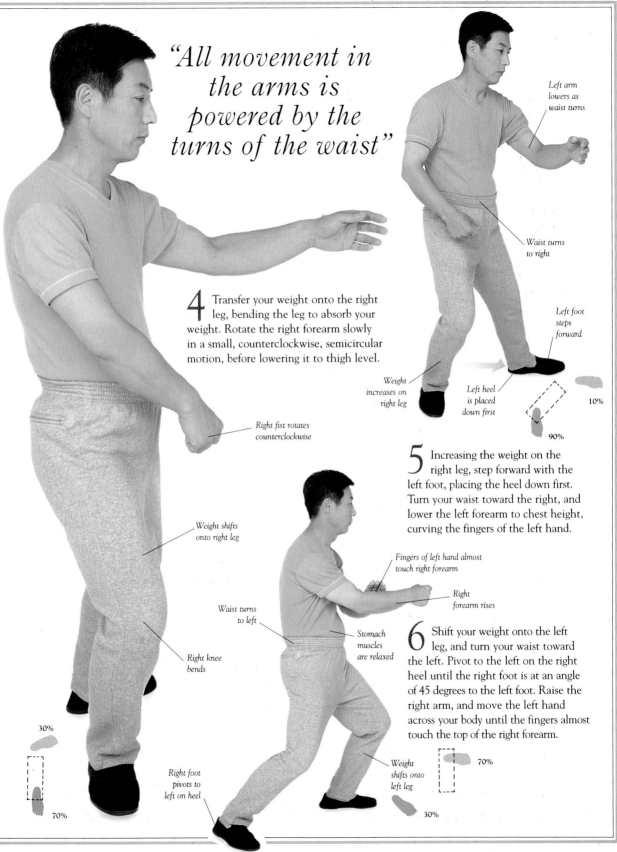

"All movement in the arms is powered by the turns of the waist"

Left arm lowers as waist turns

Waist turns to right

Left foot steps forward

4 Transfer your weight onto the right leg, bending the leg to absorb your weight. Rotate the right forearm slowly in a small, counterclockwise, semicircular motion, before lowering it to thigh level.

Weight increases on right leg

Left heel is placed down first

10%

90%

Right fist rotates counterclockwise

5 Increasing the weight on the right leg, step forward with the left foot, placing the heel down first. Turn your waist toward the right, and lower the left forearm to chest height, curving the fingers of the left hand.

Weight shifts onto right leg

Fingers of left hand almost touch right forearm

Right forearm rises

Waist turns to left

Stomach muscles are relaxed

6 Shift your weight onto the left leg, and turn your waist toward the left. Pivot to the left on the right heel until the right foot is at an angle of 45 degrees to the left foot. Raise the right arm, and move the left hand across your body until the fingers almost touch the top of the right forearm.

Right knee bends

30%

70%

Right foot pivots to left on heel

Weight shifts onto left leg

70%

30%

APPERENT CLOSE-UP

如封似閉

Also called as *As If Closing a Door*, this sequence trains the body to move from the waist without using the feet. This is an important skill in pushing hands and application, creating the perfect counter to a trap or grab when combined with the placing of the left hand beneath the right elbow. The closing up, or crossing of the arms, making an apparently vulnerable position, is turned into a strong position by the subtle body movement back, and then forward. The application on page 114 demonstrates the hidden shift from defense to attack in this movement.

1 Start to shift your weight onto the right leg, and position the left hand beneath the right elbow, with the fingers pointing to the right and the palm facing upward.

Weight begins to shift onto right leg

Left palm is below right elbow

60%

40%

2 Increase the weight on the right leg, sitting farther back as you shift the weight backward. Cross the forearms over at the wrists, placing the left forearm beneath the right wrist.

Left forearm brushes right forearm

40%

60%

Fingers are outstretched

Arm is in Push position

Weight increases on right leg

3 Shift some weight onto the right leg, sitting back farther. Uncross the arms, and hold them parallel, the fingers extended, and the palms facing out and downward.

30%

70%

Left leg almost straightens

Weight increases further on right leg

4 Shift your weight onto the left leg. With the forearms parallel and palms facing downward, move the upper body forward into the *Push* position (see p. 29).

Left knee bends

Weight shifts onto left leg

70%

30%

PREVIOUS STAGES

└ p. 36 ┘   └ Brush Knee, Twist Step, p. 37 ┘   └─────── Step Forward, Move, Parry, and Punch, p. 38 ───────

十字手 CROSS HANDS

The object of this sequence of movements, which is repeated near the end of the form, is to adjust posture without losing stability. The key to this is to root down through the left leg at the end of the sequence, although the weight will appear to be evenly distributed through both legs. This is one of the few instances in the form in which the body weight appears to fall equally through both legs – a fault known as double weighting. Normally, weight is rooted very decisively and obviously through one leg or the other, which is usually necessary if a firm stance is to be maintained.

1 Shift most of your weight onto the right leg, and straighten the left leg as you move. Turn your waist and both arms to the right at the same time.

Fingers point down slightly

Waist turns to right

Weight shifts onto right leg

Arm rises

Waist turns farther to right

20%

80%

APPLICATION

Defender's right hand forms palm strike

Defender

Opponent

To intercept an opponent's right-handed punch to the side of the head, the defender pivots to the right on the left foot to face the opponent. In order to deflect the incoming punch with his left wrist, he opens and raises his arms to shoulder height in *Cross Hands*, and strikes the opponent on the chest with the palm of his right hand.

2 Transfer most of your weight onto the left leg, and turn the toes of the right foot inward. Pivot 90 degrees to the right on the left heel until the left foot faces forward. Raise both arms to shoulder height.

Arm swings across chest

Fingers face outward

Weight shifts onto left leg

Arm rises to shoulder height

Toes of right foot turn inward

80%

20%

40%

60%

3 Move the arms backward, bend the forearms upward, and turn the fingers of both hands outward. Pivot on the right heel to the right, and step backward with the right foot, positioning it about a shoulders' width from the left.

20%

80%

Right leg moves backward

Right foot steps backward

4 Lower the arms to waist level, and swing them up across your chest, crossing the wrists with the left hand closest to your body. Leave a space under each armpit, and also between the arms and chest.

抱虎歸山 EMBRACE TIGER, RETURN TO MOUNTAIN

Much of the power in this sequence comes from the movement of the waist, with both arms following its rolling action, so that the whole of the upper body is moving as a single unit. The movement also illustrates two of the most fundamental principles of t'ai chi; firstly, that when the limbs and body act together, moving in unison, they have considerably more power than when moving in isolation, and secondly, how to change direction to deflect and unbalance an approaching attacker.

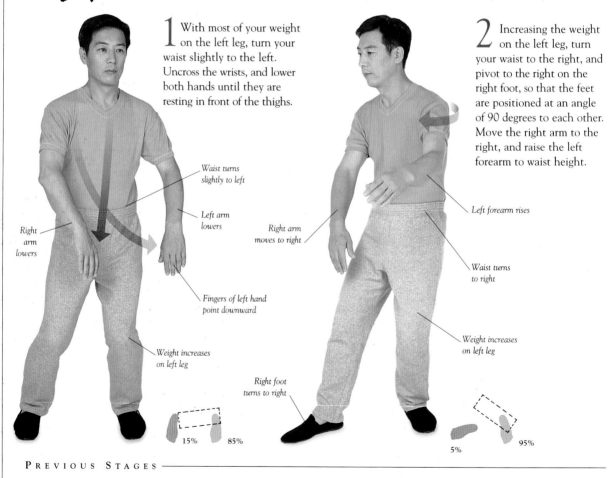

1 With most of your weight on the left leg, turn your waist slightly to the left. Uncross the wrists, and lower both hands until they are resting in front of the thighs.

Waist turns slightly to left

Left arm lowers

Right arm lowers

Fingers of left hand point downward

Weight increases on left leg

15%　85%

2 Increasing the weight on the left leg, turn your waist to the right, and pivot to the right on the right foot, so that the feet are positioned at an angle of 90 degrees to each other. Move the right arm to the right, and raise the left forearm to waist height.

Left forearm rises

Right arm moves to right

Waist turns to right

Weight increases on left leg

Right foot turns to right

5%　95%

PREVIOUS STAGES

└── p. 39 ──┘　└── Apparent Close-Up, p. 40 ──┘　└── Cross Hands, p. 41 ──┘

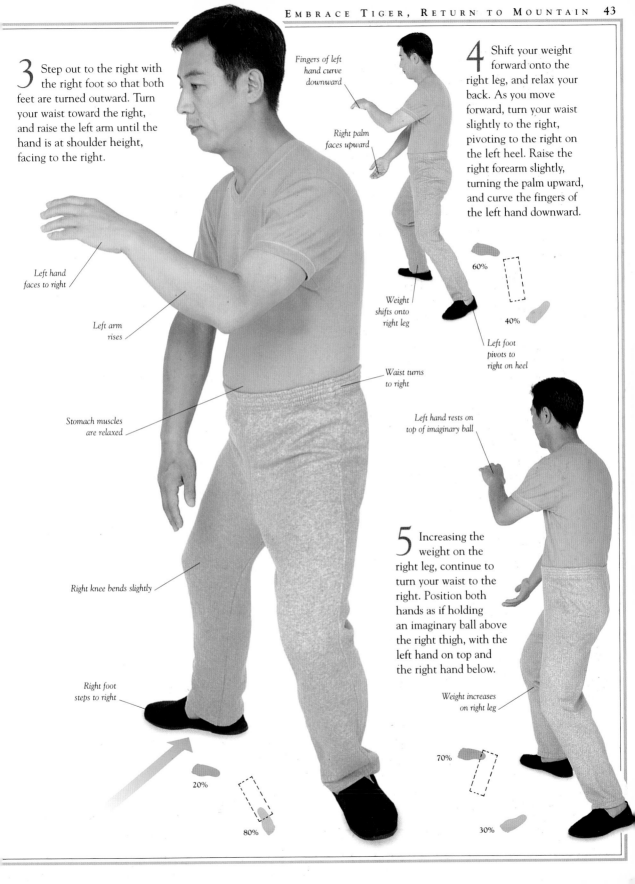

3 Step out to the right with the right foot so that both feet are turned outward. Turn your waist toward the right, and raise the left arm until the hand is at shoulder height, facing to the right.

Fingers of left hand curve downward

Right palm faces upward

4 Shift your weight forward onto the right leg, and relax your back. As you move forward, turn your waist slightly to the right, pivoting to the right on the left heel. Raise the right forearm slightly, turning the palm upward, and curve the fingers of the left hand downward.

Left hand faces to right

Left arm rises

Stomach muscles are relaxed

Waist turns to right

Weight shifts onto right leg

60%

40%

Left foot pivots to right on heel

Left hand rests on top of imaginary ball

5 Increasing the weight on the right leg, continue to turn your waist to the right. Position both hands as if holding an imaginary ball above the right thigh, with the left hand on top and the right hand below.

Right knee bends slightly

Right foot steps to right

Weight increases on right leg

20%

80%

70%

30%

掤 撮 擠 按 WARD-OFF, ROLL BACK, PRESS, AND PUSH

This sequence repeats a number of familiar movements, and it provides an opportunity to relax the hip joints and test the mobility of the waist by turning it from side to side. The previous sequence (see p. 43) ended with most of the power stored in the right leg, all of which is released during *Ward-Off*, which enables the leg to relax. An increase in the energy stored in the body is felt during the execution of the *Roll Back* section of this sequence.

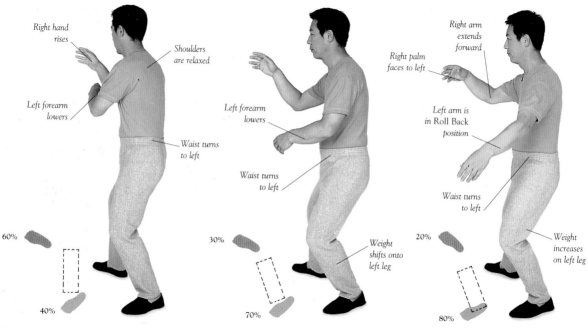

Right hand rises
Shoulders are relaxed
Left forearm lowers
Waist turns to left
60%
40%

Left forearm lowers
Waist turns to left
Weight shifts onto left leg
30%
70%

Right arm extends forward
Right palm faces to left
Left arm is in Roll Back position
Waist turns to left
Weight increases on left leg
20%
80%

1 Shift some of your weight onto the left leg, and start to turn your waist to the left. At the same time, raise the right hand to shoulder height, with the palm facing to the left. Lower the left forearm across your chest, with the palm facing inward.

2 Sitting farther back on the left leg, turn your waist farther to the left, keeping the lower body relaxed to help the rolling action of your waist. Move both arms to the left as your body moves, and lower the left forearm so that it rests at waist height.

3 Continue to turn to the left into the *Roll Back* position, lowering the left forearm, with the palm facing to the right. Begin to extend the right forearm slightly forward, with the fingers of the right hand curved, and the palm facing to the left.

PREVIOUS STAGES

└ p. 40 ┘ └ Cross Hands, p. 41 ┘ └ Embrace Tiger, Return to Mountain, p. 42 ┘

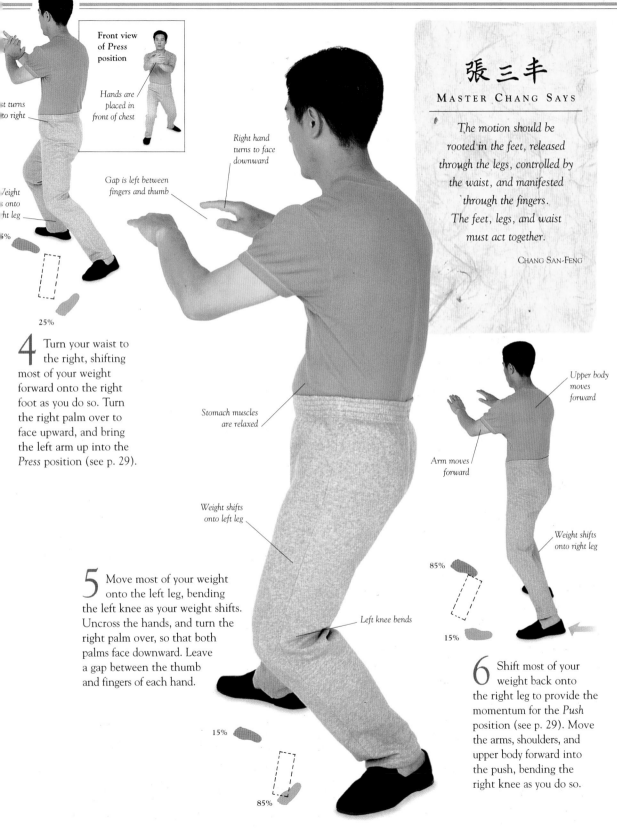

Front view of Press position

Hands are placed in front of chest

st turns to right

Veight s onto ht leg

5%

25%

Right hand turns to face downward

Gap is left between fingers and thumb

張三丰

MASTER CHANG SAYS

The motion should be rooted in the feet, released through the legs, controlled by the waist, and manifested through the fingers. The feet, legs, and waist must act together.

CHANG SAN-FENG

Stomach muscles are relaxed

Upper body moves forward

Arm moves forward

Weight shifts onto right leg

4 Turn your waist to the right, shifting most of your weight forward onto the right foot as you do so. Turn the right palm over to face upward, and bring the left arm up into the Press position (see p. 29).

Weight shifts onto left leg

Left knee bends

85%

15%

5 Move most of your weight onto the left leg, bending the left knee as your weight shifts. Uncross the hands, and turn the right palm over, so that both palms face downward. Leave a gap between the thumb and fingers of each hand.

15%

85%

6 Shift most of your weight back onto the right leg to provide the momentum for the Push position (see p. 29). Move the arms, shoulders, and upper body forward into the push, bending the right knee as you do so.

轉身掉手 TURN THE BODY, AND LOWER THE HANDS

Some would regard this movement as part of *Diagonal Single Whip* (see opposite), others as a connecting posture added to Cheng Man-ch'ing's original form to facilitate a smooth transition from the previous stances to *Diagonal Single Whip*. Whatever its origin, *Turn the Body, and Lower the Hands* precedes all five *Single Whip* sequences in the form, establishing a strong root and providing a stable base from which to gather energy for the next posture.

Upper back is relaxed

Lower back is rounded

Waist turns to left

Forearm is parallel with floor

Weight shifts onto left leg

20%

80%

Arm rotates with waist

Waist turns to left

10%

90%

Right hand rests on imaginary ball

Back is rounded

Waist turns to right

Left hand supports imaginary ball

Weight shifts onto right leg

80%

20%

1 Shift most of your weight back onto the left leg, and turn the waist to the left, bending the knees slightly and lowering the forearms to chest height.

2 Turn your waist farther to the left, keeping the arms coordinated with your waist. As you turn, root firmly down through the left leg, keeping the knees bent.

3 Shift most of your weight onto the right leg, and turn your waist to the right. Place both hands as if holding an imaginary ball above the left thigh, the right hand on top.

PREVIOUS STAGES

Embrace Tiger, Return to Mountain, p. 42 — Ward-Off, Roll Back, Press, and Push, p. 44

斜單鞭 DIAGONAL SINGLE WHIP

This series of moves is similar to the first *Single Whip* sequence (see p. 31). The major difference in this case is that the left foot steps out diagonally and forward, instead of to the left side. As in the first *Single Whip*, there should be a feeling of physical expansion across the chest and through the arms at the end of the sequence. When turning to the left, make sure that the left arm moves around in time with the waist; this can be achieved only when the weight distribution is correct.

1 Increasing the weight on the right leg, turn your waist to the left. Form a loose hook shape with the right hand, and extend it away from your body at shoulder height.

Right hand forms loose hook

Weight increases on right leg

Waist turns to left

90%

Toes of left foot point forward

10%

2 Turning your waist slightly farther to the left, take a step out to the left with the left foot. Place the heel down first, and pivot on it through an angle of 45 degrees to the left, before rolling the rest of the foot down.

Waist turns to left

Left foot pivots to left

90%

10%

Left heel is placed down first

3 Shift your weight onto the left leg, and turn your waist farther to the left. Raise the left shoulder, moving the left forearm across your body to shoulder height, with the palm facing to the right.

Left shoulder rises

Left wrist bends to right

Waist turns to left

40%

60%

Weight shifts onto left leg

4 Increasing the weight on the left leg, turn your waist farther to the left, and twist the left forearm towards the left so that the palm faces downward.

Left palm faces downward

Left forearm extends

Waist turns to left

Weight increases on left leg

30%

70%

肘底看捶 FIST UNDER ELBOW

This sequence begins with wide, expansive arm movements, which are designed to rid the shoulders, back, and upper body of tension built up in the earlier stages of the form. The actions in *Fist Under Elbow* demonstrate how to shift the body weight from one leg to the other in quick succession while moving forward. Such movements are useful in application, since they develop contact and parrying skills without loss of balance. Repeated practice of these posture changes builds up strength in the legs, aids stability, and increases the flexibility of the body.

Shoulders are relaxed

Right arm begins to move to left

Left palm faces forward

Right hand forms loose hook

Waist turns to left

Waist turns farther to left

Left arm lowers

Left leg is almost weightless

Weight increases on right leg

Left leg almost straightens

Weight shifts onto right leg

1 Shift most of your weight onto the right leg, and turn your waist to the left, straightening the left leg as your weight shifts backward. Keep both arms open, and move them to the left with your waist.

80%   20%

95%   5%

2 With nearly all your weight on the right leg, turn your waist farther to the left until the left leg is almost weightless. Keep moving both arms to the left with your waist.

PREVIOUS STAGES

Press, and Push, p. 45   Turn the Body, p. 46   Diagonal Single Whip, p. 47

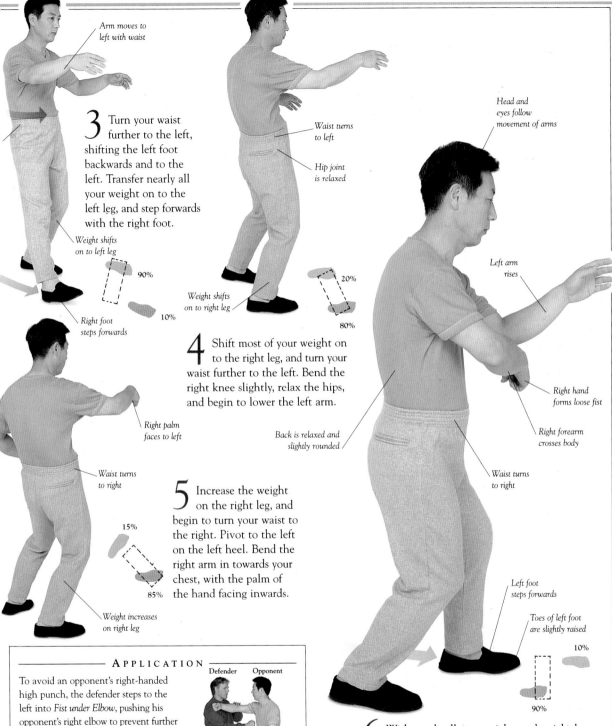

Arm moves to left with waist

3 Turn your waist further to the left, shifting the left foot backwards and to the left. Transfer nearly all your weight on to the left leg, and step forwards with the right foot.

Weight shifts on to left leg

90%

10%

Right foot steps forwards

Waist turns to left

Hip joint is relaxed

Weight shifts on to right leg

20%

80%

4 Shift most of your weight on to the right leg, and turn your waist further to the left. Bend the right knee slightly, relax the hips, and begin to lower the left arm.

Head and eyes follow movement of arms

Left arm rises

Right hand forms loose fist

Right forearm crosses body

Waist turns to right

Right palm faces to left

Back is relaxed and slightly rounded

Waist turns to right

5 Increase the weight on the right leg, and begin to turn your waist to the right. Pivot to the left on the left heel. Bend the right arm in towards your chest, with the palm of the hand facing inwards.

15%

85%

Weight increases on right leg

Left foot steps forwards

Toes of left foot are slightly raised

10%

90%

6 With nearly all your weight on the right leg, turn your waist further to the right, and step forwards with the left foot, placing the left heel down first. Raise the left arm, and lower the right arm in front of your body, forming a loose fist with the right hand, resting it under the left elbow.

APPLICATION

To avoid an opponent's right-handed high punch, the defender steps to the left into *Fist under Elbow*, pushing his opponent's right elbow to prevent further threat. Shifting his weight on to the right leg, the defender sits back, and delivers a punch to the opponent's ribs. To increase the power of the punch, the defender shifts his weight forwards.

Defender   Opponent

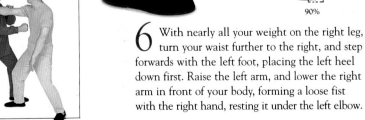

Weight shifts on to right leg

倒撵猴 STEP BACK TO REPULSE THE MONKEY *I*

A long sequence that is shown over the following four pages, *Step Back to Repulse the Monkey* is a valuable aid to teaching balance, stability, and coordination while stepping backward. It is frequently used in application practice (see p. 114), when the extended arm maintains contact with the opponent, and holds them at bay so that a retreat can be made to create space for a countermove. As always when practicing with a partner, the defender should be able to judge the opponent's lack of balance.

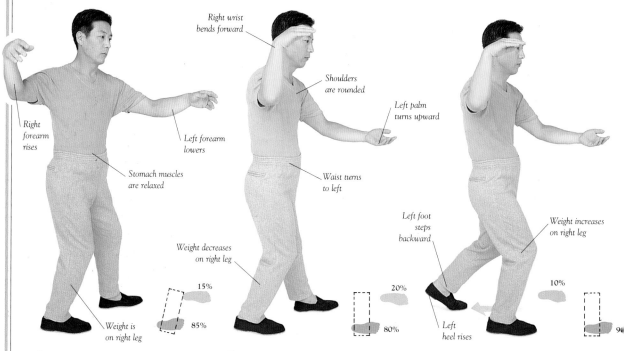

Right wrist bends forward

Shoulders are rounded

Left palm turns upward

Right forearm rises

Left forearm lowers

Stomach muscles are relaxed

Waist turns to left

Left foot steps backward

Weight increases on right leg

Weight decreases on right leg

15%

85%

20%

80%

10%

9[

Weight is on right leg

Left heel rises

1 Turning your waist to the right, lower the left forearm, and extend it forward. Lower the right hand to the right in a circular motion past the right hip, raising it to shoulder height, with the fingers extended.

2 Placing a little more weight on the left leg, turn the waist to the left. Lower the left forearm to waist level, turning the palm upward. Move the right forearm inward, bend the wrist forward, and raise the hand to ear level.

3 With a little more weight back on the right leg, step backward with the left foot, putting the toes of the foot down first, before rolling down onto the heel. Keep both legs bent, and sink your body slightly.

PREVIOUS STAGES

Diagonal Single Whip, p. 47

Fist Under Elbow, p. 48

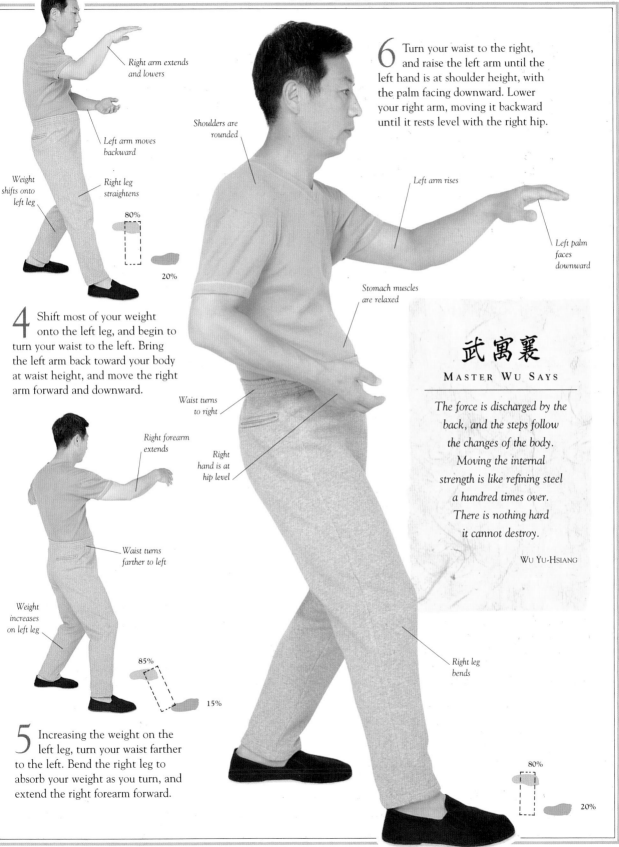

Right arm extends
and lowers

Left arm moves
backward

Weight
shifts onto
left leg

Right leg
straightens

80%

20%

4 Shift most of your weight
onto the left leg, and begin to
turn your waist to the left. Bring
the left arm back toward your body
at waist height, and move the right
arm forward and downward.

Right forearm
extends

Waist turns
farther to left

Weight
increases
on left leg

85%

15%

5 Increasing the weight on the
left leg, turn your waist farther
to the left. Bend the right leg to
absorb your weight as you turn, and
extend the right forearm forward.

Shoulders are
rounded

Left arm rises

Left palm
faces
downward

Stomach muscles
are relaxed

Waist turns
to right

Right
hand is at
hip level

Right leg
bends

6 Turn your waist to the right,
and raise the left arm until the
left hand is at shoulder height, with
the palm facing downward. Lower
your right arm, moving it backward
until it rests level with the right hip.

武寓襄

MASTER WU SAYS

*The force is discharged by the
back, and the steps follow
the changes of the body.
Moving the internal
strength is like refining steel
a hundred times over.
There is nothing hard
it cannot destroy.*

WU YU-HSIANG

80%

20%

STEP BACK TO REPULSE THE MONKEY II

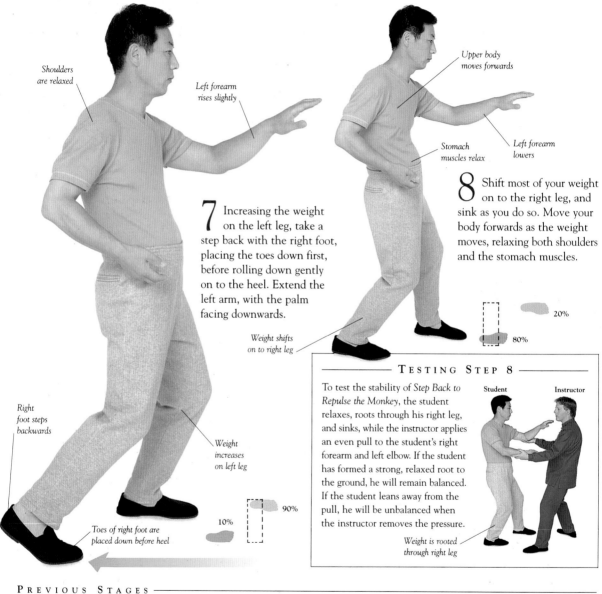

Shoulders
are relaxed

Left forearm
rises slightly

Upper body
moves forwards

Stomach
muscles relax

Left forearm
lowers

7 Increasing the weight on the left leg, take a step back with the right foot, placing the toes down first, before rolling down gently on to the heel. Extend the left arm, with the palm facing downwards.

8 Shift most of your weight on to the right leg, and sink as you do so. Move your body forwards as the weight moves, relaxing both shoulders and the stomach muscles.

Weight shifts
on to right leg

20%

80%

Right
foot steps
backwards

Weight
increases
on left leg

Toes of right foot are
placed down before heel

10%

90%

TESTING STEP 8

To test the stability of *Step Back to Repulse the Monkey*, the student relaxes, roots through his right leg, and sinks, while the instructor applies an even pull to the student's right forearm and left elbow. If the student has formed a strong, relaxed root to the ground, he will remain balanced. If the student leans away from the pull, he will be unbalanced when the instructor removes the pressure.

Student   Instructor

Weight is rooted
through right leg

PREVIOUS STAGES

Fist under Elbow, p. 48

Step Back to Repulse the Monkey I, p. 50

Left palm
faces right

Waist turns
to right

Right
arm
rises

Weight
eases
right leg

15%

85%

9 Turn your waist to the right, and twist the left arm slightly so that the palm is facing to the right. Raise the right forearm to chin height.

"The connection to the ground through the feet is vital in T'ai chi"

11 Take a step backwards with the left foot, placing the toes down first, then rolling down on to the heel. Keeping both legs bent, begin to transfer your weight backwards on to the left leg.

Right hand is level
with right ear

Left palm
faces upwards

Waist turns
to left

15%

85%

10 Turn your waist back towards the left, and turn the left palm upwards. Bring the right arm up and inwards until the hand is in line with the right ear, with the palm facing downwards and the fingers slightly raised.

Left
foot steps
backwards

20%

80%

Right
arm moves
forwards

Left hand rests
by left hip

Weight
shifts on
to left leg

80%

20%

12 Shift most of your weight on to the left leg, and lower the left forearm so that the hand rests by the left hip, with the palm facing upwards. Extend the right arm forwards from the shoulder.

斜飛勢 DIAGONAL FLYING

The overall feeling of this sequence should be of slow, controlled stretching. Although the body appears to be relaxed, it should actually be in a state of acute anticipation. The movements in the *Diagonal Flying* sequence demonstrate the technique of "splitting," which is the ability to absorb force from an attack in one direction, and exert energy to combat the attack from another. The sequence is the basis for several pushing hands drills and applications (see p. 108).

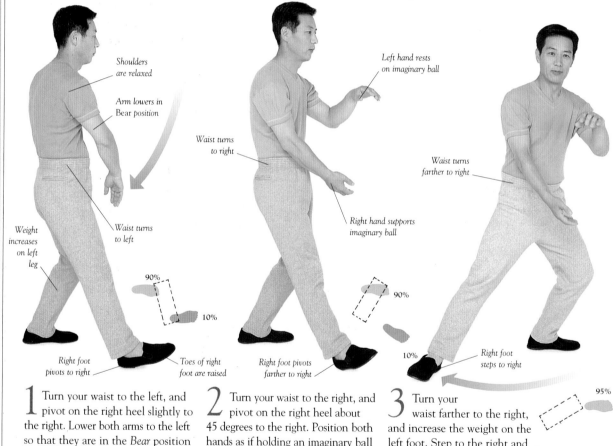

Shoulders are relaxed

Arm lowers in Bear position

Left hand rests on imaginary ball

Waist turns to right

Waist turns farther to right

Weight increases on left leg

Waist turns to left

Right hand supports imaginary ball

90%

10%

90%

10%

95%

5%

Right foot pivots to right

Toes of right foot are raised

Right foot pivots farther to right

Right foot steps to right

1 Turn your waist to the left, and pivot on the right heel slightly to the right. Lower both arms to the left so that they are in the *Bear* position (see p. 35), with the palms facing each other, and raise the left arm.

2 Turn your waist to the right, and pivot on the right heel about 45 degrees to the right. Position both hands as if holding an imaginary ball above the right thigh, with the left hand on top and the right below.

3 Turn your waist farther to the right, and increase the weight on the left foot. Step to the right and sideways with your right foot, placing the heel down first.

PREVIOUS STAGES

Step Back to Repulse the Monkey I, p. 50 ——— Step Back to Repulse the Monkey II, p. 52

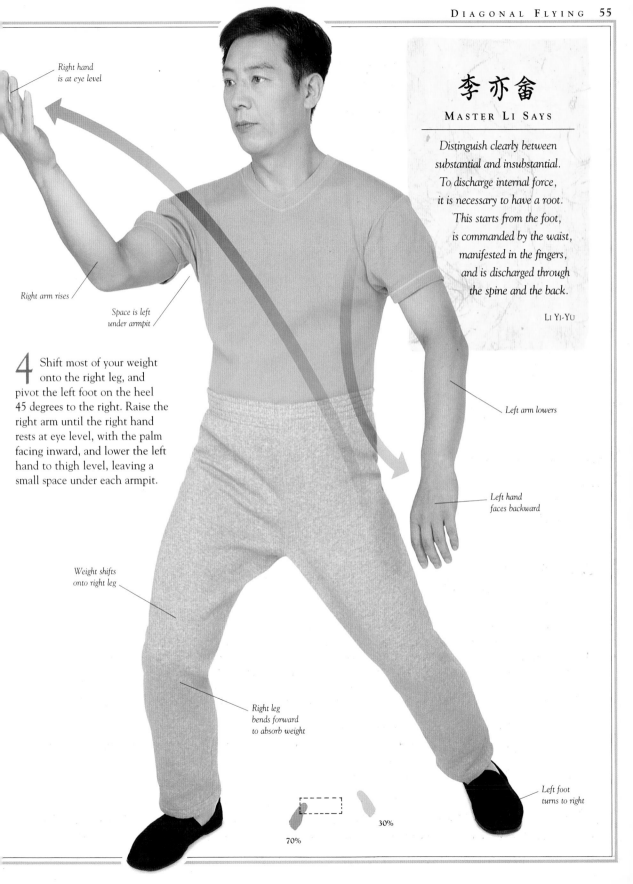

Right hand is at eye level

Right arm rises

Space is left under armpit

李亦畬

MASTER LI SAYS

Distinguish clearly between substantial and insubstantial. To discharge internal force, it is necessary to have a root. This starts from the foot, is commanded by the waist, manifested in the fingers, and is discharged through the spine and the back.

LI YI-YU

Left arm lowers

Left hand faces backward

4 Shift most of your weight onto the right leg, and pivot the left foot on the heel 45 degrees to the right. Raise the right arm until the right hand rests at eye level, with the palm facing inward, and lower the left hand to thigh level, leaving a small space under each armpit.

Weight shifts onto right leg

Right leg bends forward to absorb weight

Left foot turns to right

30%

70%

雲手 CLOUD HANDS I

The main objective of this complex sequence, which is illustrated over the next four pages, is to coordinate repeated shifts in body weight with turns powered from the waist. This leads to the development of great strength in the torso, as well as to improvements in balance and stability. Practising the simple *Bear* position (see p. 35), helps the performance of *Cloud Hands*, since the movement of the waist and upper body from side to side is similar in both instances. It is vital to be relaxed so that the hips are flexible enough to swing smoothly from side to side.

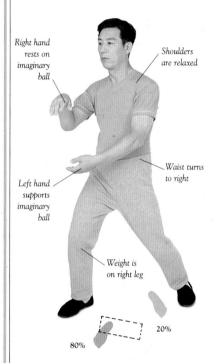

Right hand rests on imaginary ball

Shoulders are relaxed

Waist turns to right

Left hand supports imaginary ball

Weight is on right leg

80%   20%

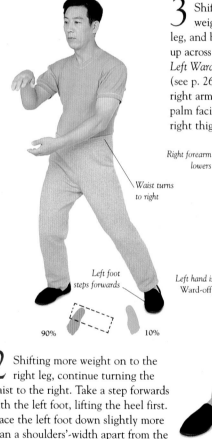

Waist turns to right

Left foot steps forwards

90%   10%

3 Shift most of your weight on to the left leg, and bring the left arm up across your body in the *Left Ward-off* position (see p. 26). Lower the right arm, with the palm facing the right thigh.

Right forearm lowers

Left hand is in Left Ward-off position

Weight shifts on to left leg

20%   80%

1 Keeping most of your weight on the right leg, turn your waist to the right, and move the right hand down to just below the right shoulder. Lift the left hand, and position both hands as if holding an imaginary ball above the right thigh, with the right hand on top.

2 Shifting more weight on to the right leg, continue turning the waist to the right. Take a step forwards with the left foot, lifting the heel first. Place the left foot down slightly more than a shoulders'-width apart from the right foot, with the toes almost in line.

PREVIOUS STAGES

Step Back to Repulse the Monkey II, p. 52   Diagonal Flying, p. 54

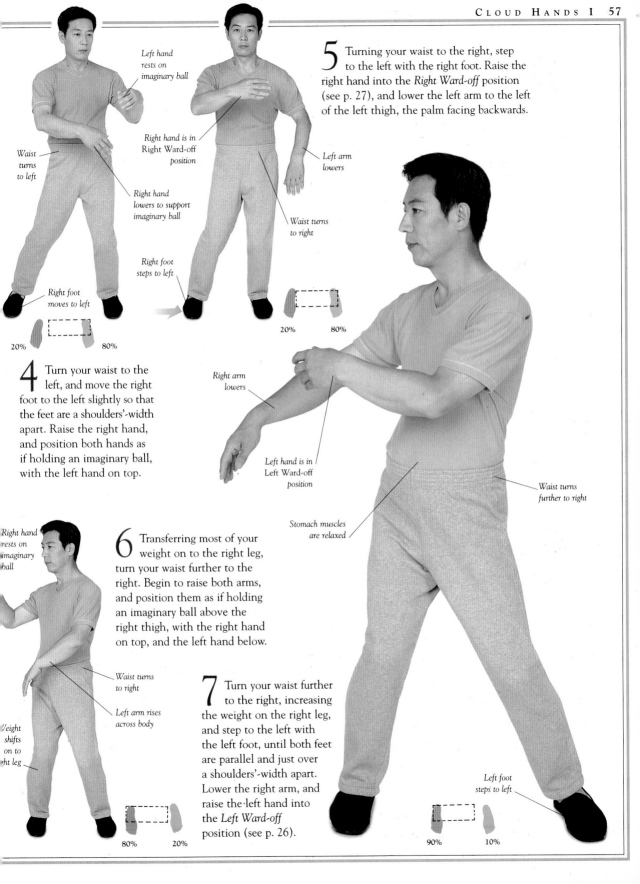

Left hand
rests on
imaginary ball

Right hand is in
Right Ward-off
position

Waist
turns
to left

Right hand
lowers to support
imaginary ball

Left arm
lowers

Waist turns
to right

Right foot
steps to left

Right foot
moves to left

20%   80%

20%   80%

5 Turning your waist to the right, step to the left with the right foot. Raise the right hand into the *Right Ward-off* position (see p. 27), and lower the left arm to the left of the left thigh, the palm facing backwards.

4 Turn your waist to the left, and move the right foot to the left slightly so that the feet are a shoulders'-width apart. Raise the right hand, and position both hands as if holding an imaginary ball, with the left hand on top.

Right arm
lowers

Left hand is in
Left Ward-off
position

Stomach muscles
are relaxed

Waist turns
further to right

Right hand
rests on
imaginary
ball

6 Transferring most of your weight on to the right leg, turn your waist further to the right. Begin to raise both arms, and position them as if holding an imaginary ball above the right thigh, with the right hand on top, and the left hand below.

Waist turns
to right

Left arm rises
across body

Weight
shifts
on to
right leg

7 Turn your waist further to the right, increasing the weight on the right leg, and step to the left with the left foot, until both feet are parallel and just over a shoulders'-width apart. Lower the right arm, and raise the left hand into the *Left Ward-off* position (see p. 26).

Left foot
steps to left

80%   20%

90%   10%

CLOUD HANDS II

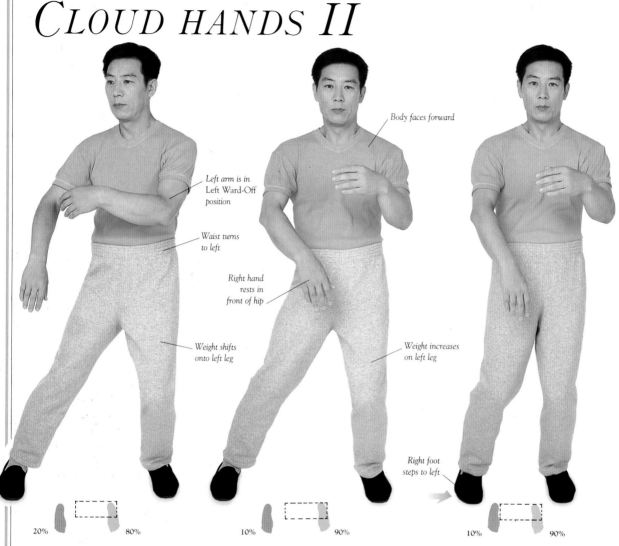

Left arm is in Left Ward-Off position

Waist turns to left

Weight shifts onto left leg

20%   80%

Body faces forward

Right hand rests in front of hip

Weight increases on left leg

10%   90%

Right foot steps to left

10%   90%

8 Transfer most of your weight onto the left leg and, as you do so, turn your waist slightly to the left. At the same time, move both arms to the left with the body until they are in the *Left Ward-Off* position (see p. 26).

9 Increase the weight on the left leg, and continue turning your waist to the left until your body faces forward. Move the right hand in front of the right hip, and slightly raise the left forearm to chest height.

10 Take a small step to the left with the right foot until it is about a shoulders' width away from the left foot, with the toes of both feet facing forward. Relax, and feel the strong root through the left leg.

PREVIOUS STAGES

Diagonal Flying, p. 54   Cloud Hands I, p. 56

Right arm is in relaxed Right Ward-Off position

Left arm lowers

Waist turns to right

Weight shifts onto right leg

Left foot steps to left

90%   10%

Body faces forward

Right arm lowers

Space is left under armpit

Left arm is in Left Ward-Off position

Left hand rests on imaginary ball

Right hand moves to support imaginary ball

Right foot steps forward

95%   5%

11 Shifting nearly all your weight onto the right leg, turn your waist to the right. Take a step out to the left with the left foot until the feet are just over a shoulders' width apart. As you turn, raise the right arm in *Right Ward-Off* (see p. 27), and lower the left arm across your chest.

13 Take a small step forward with the right foot. With the left hand at chest height, position the hands as if holding an imaginary ball above the left thigh, with the left hand on top and the right hand below.

12 Transfer most of your weight onto the left leg, and turn your waist to the left until you face forward. Move both arms to the left, and raise the left arm in *Left Ward-Off* (see p. 26), lowering the right arm to thigh level.

20%   80%

Weight shifts onto left leg

Right arm is in Right Ward-Off position

Space is left under armpit

Left hand rests by left thigh

14 Shift most of your weight forward onto the right leg, and bring the right arm up into the *Right Ward-Off* position. Lower the left hand to rest by the left thigh, and leave a space under each armpit.

Weight shifts onto right leg

20%   80%

單鞭下勢 DESCENDING SINGLE WHIP

This is the second *Single Whip* sequence in the Form, and is often known as *Snake Creeps Down*, a name that reflects the slow, sinking action required in the postures at the end of the sequence. The stance in Step Four of this sequence resembles the final posture of the previous *Single Whip* sequence (see p. 31), but should be wider to facilitate the final descent, which requires considerable flexibility and balance. This is helped by the right foot pivoting to the right in Step Five, relaxing the right hip joint to provide further stability. Such an apparently small adjustment of the foot can have a major effect on the balance during the descent.

Right hand forms loose hook

Right arm rises

Right hand rests on imaginary ball

Left hand supports imaginary ball

Weight increases on right leg

15%

85%

1 Increase the weight on the right leg, turn your waist to the right, and turn the left foot to the left. Position both hands as if holding an imaginary ball above the right thigh, with the right hand on top.

Left hand rests at waist height

Waist turns to left

Left foot turns to left

15%

85%

95%

2 Turn your waist to the left, and turn the left foot further to the left. Raise the right hand to shoulder height, forming a loose hook shape (see p. 31), and turn the left palm inwards, holding the left forearm at hip level.

Right arm moves to left with body

3 With nearly all your weight on the right leg, turn your waist further to the left, moving both arms to the left as your waist moves. Take a wide step to the left with the left foot.

Waist turns further to left

Weight increases on right leg

5%

Left leg is almost weightless

Left foot steps to left

PREVIOUS STAGES

Cloud Hands I, p. 56

Cloud Hands II, p. 58

Right arm moves with waist

Left arm rises

Palm faces downwards

Waist turns to left

Knee is bent and relaxed

4 Turn your waist further to the left, and raise the left arm until the hand is at shoulder level. Pivot on the right heel through an angle of 45 degrees to the left, until you are in the *Single Whip* position (see p. 31).

Right foot pivots to left on heel

30%

70%

Waist turns to right

Weight increases on left leg

Right foot pivots to right on heel

5 Transfer most of your weight on to the left leg, and turn your waist to the right. Pivot on the right heel through an angle of 45 degrees to the right, so that your stance is stable and wide for the descent.

85%

15%

Eyes follow movement of left hand

Right arm extends sideways

Waist turns to left

Left palm faces right

Left arm lowers as body sinks

Front view of Descending Single Whip

Left leg is slightly bent

Weight increases on right leg

30%

70%

6 Shift your weight on to the right leg, and begin to descend by bending the right knee. At the same time, turn the left forearm to face the right, and move it downwards as you sink.

Weight increases on right leg

25%

75%

Left leg extends

Toes of left foot turn to right

7 With most of your weight on the right leg, extend the right arm at shoulder height, and descend slowly. Bend the right knee until the left leg is extended, and turn your waist slightly to the left, tilting your head downwards. Turn the toes of the left foot to the right to provide extra stability.

金
鷄
獨
立

GOLDEN ROOSTER STANDS ON ONE LEG

This sequence tests the strength and stability of the root by shifting weight from one leg to the other, and complements the downward movement of *Descending Single Whip* (see p. 60) with an upward motion. The key to executing the move successfully is in coordinating the arms and legs, and not rising too high or sinking too low.

1 Turn the left foot slightly to the right on the heel, keeping the foot in line with the left arm. Rise, and begin to raise the left forearm. Bend the left knee forward, shift some weight onto the left leg, and pivot the right foot to the left.

Right hand forms loose hook

Left forearm rises

Weight increases on left leg

Right foot pivots to left

Left foot turns to right

60%

40%

Left palm faces downward

Left forearm rises

Right arm moves forward

Weight shifts onto left leg

2 Shift nearly all your weight onto the left leg, and raise the left arm, with the palm facing downward. Step forward onto the toes of the right foot, lower the right arm forward, and extend the fingers downward.

Right heel is raised

Right foot steps forward

90%

10%

PREVIOUS STAGES

Cloud Hands II, p. 58 ———   Descending Single Whip, p. 60

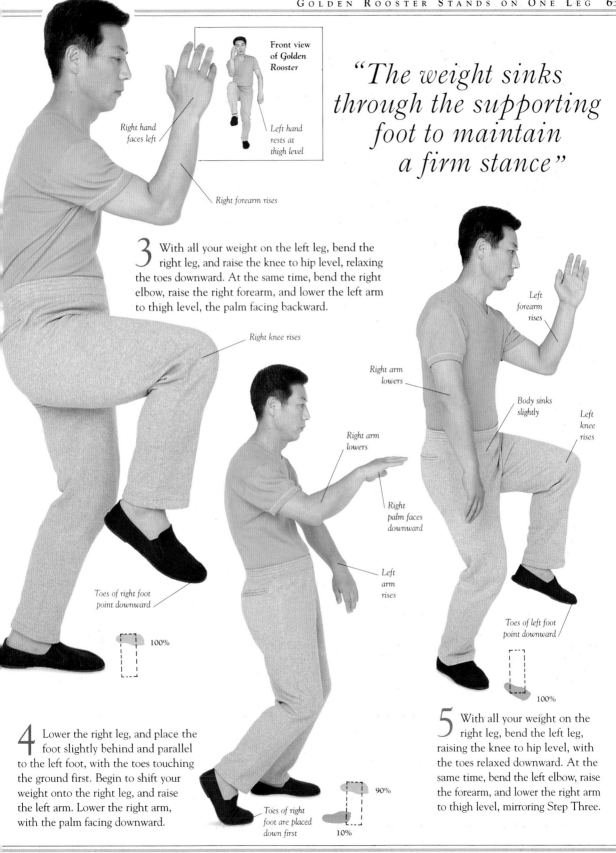

Front view
of Golden
Rooster

Right hand
faces left

Left hand
rests at
thigh level

Right forearm rises

"The weight sinks through the supporting foot to maintain a firm stance"

3 With all your weight on the left leg, bend the right leg, and raise the knee to hip level, relaxing the toes downward. At the same time, bend the right elbow, raise the right forearm, and lower the left arm to thigh level, the palm facing backward.

Left
forearm
rises

Right knee rises

Right arm
lowers

Right arm
lowers

Body sinks
slightly

Left
knee
rises

Right
palm faces
downward

Left
arm
rises

Toes of right foot
point downward

100%

Toes of left foot
point downward

100%

4 Lower the right leg, and place the foot slightly behind and parallel to the left foot, with the toes touching the ground first. Begin to shift your weight onto the right leg, and raise the left arm. Lower the right arm, with the palm facing downward.

Toes of right
foot are placed
down first

90%

10%

5 With all your weight on the right leg, bend the left leg, raising the knee to hip level, with the toes relaxed downward. At the same time, bend the left elbow, raise the forearm, and lower the right arm to thigh level, mirroring Step Three.

右分脚 RIGHT TOE KICK

The literal translation of the Chinese term for this sequence is *Separate Right Foot*. It is the first of three sequences that end in kicks, and like the others must be practised according to the fundamental principles of T'ai chi: all movement should be as relaxed, stable, and controlled as possible, so that the kick is not too high. Although weight is rooted through the supporting leg, the kicking leg should be sufficiently relaxed to feel heavy; to achieve this the hip joints must be flexible and loose. This sequence incorporates the key elements of *Ward-off* and *Roll Back* in Steps Two and Three.

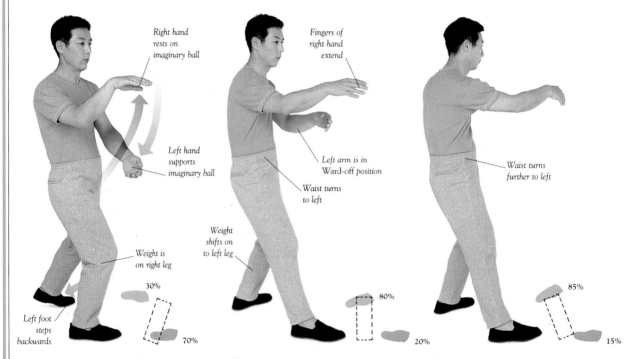

Right hand
rests on
imaginary ball

Left hand
supports
imaginary ball

Weight is
on right leg

Left foot
steps
backwards

30%

70%

Fingers of
right hand
extend

Left arm is in
Ward-off position

Waist turns
to left

Weight
shifts on
to left leg

80%

20%

Waist turns
further to left

85%

15%

1 Step backwards and left on the left foot, placing the toes down first. Lift the right arm, and lower the left arm across your body. Position the hands as if holding an imaginary ball in front of the right thigh, with the right hand on top.

2 Shift most of your weight on to the left leg, and turn your waist to the left. Raise the left arm towards the chest, and extend the right arm forwards at shoulder height, to form the left *Ward-off* position (see p. 26).

3 Increasing the weight on your left leg, turn your waist further to the left, and roll the right forearm inwards. Lower the left arm until it is at thigh level, with the palm facing forwards, in the *Roll Back* position (see p. 28).

PREVIOUS STAGES

Descending Single Whip, p. 60 ———

Golden Rooster Stands on One Leg, p. 62 ———

Defender   Opponent

Torso is pushed backward

Right leg is in Right Toe Kick

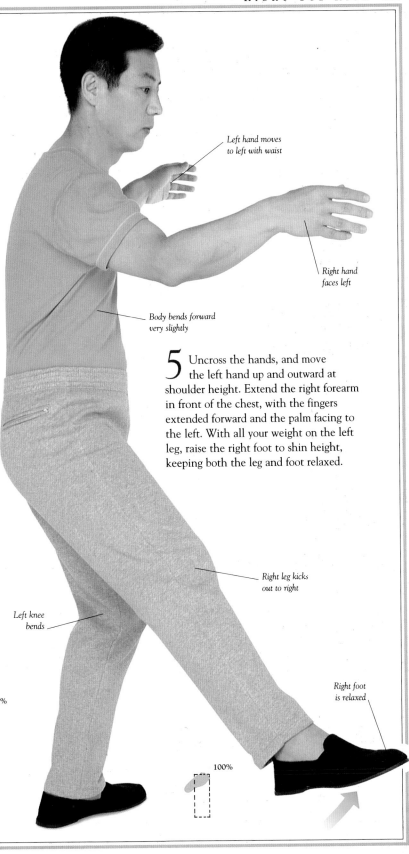

Left hand moves to left with waist

Right hand faces left

Body bends forward very slightly

5 Uncross the hands, and move the left hand up and outward at shoulder height. Extend the right forearm in front of the chest, with the fingers extended forward and the palm facing to the left. With all your weight on the left leg, raise the right foot to shin height, keeping both the leg and foot relaxed.

Right leg kicks out to right

Left knee bends

Right foot is relaxed

100%

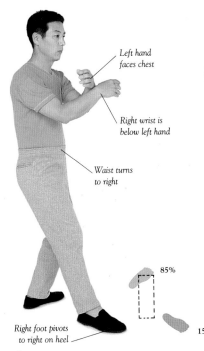

Left hand faces chest

Right wrist is below left hand

Waist turns to right

85%

15%

Right foot pivots to right on heel

4 Turn your waist to the right, pivot to the right on the right heel, and raise the left arm to chest height, moving it in a small, circular motion to the left. Bring it to rest on the top of the right wrist, and turn both palms in toward the chest.

左分脚 LEFT TOE KICK

In t'ai chi, one sequence of movements is often complemented by the next. Here, *Left Toe Kick* is the mirror image of *Right Toe Kick* (see p. 64), with the root and kick performed on opposite legs. A solid root should be formed through the right leg, and it is important not to overreach with the left leg when kicking to the side in the final posture, since this will lead to loss of stability. The main focus should be on maintaining stability when performing the kick, and for this reason it is important for beginners not to kick too high when first learning.

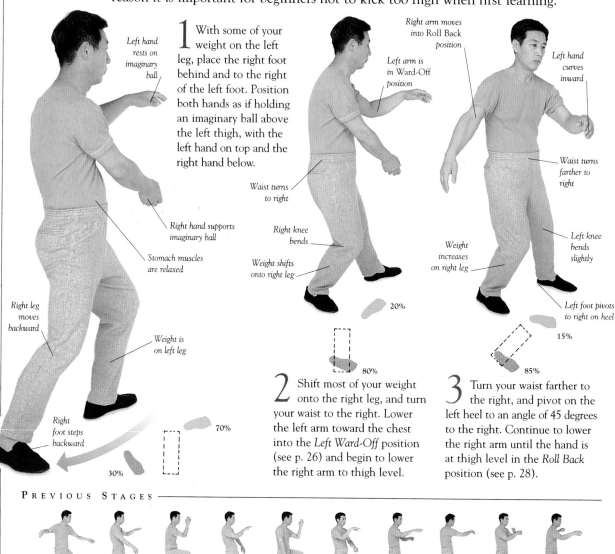

1 With some of your weight on the left leg, place the right foot behind and to the right of the left foot. Position both hands as if holding an imaginary ball above the left thigh, with the left hand on top and the right hand below.

Left hand rests on imaginary ball

Right hand supports imaginary ball

Stomach muscles are relaxed

Right leg moves backward

Weight is on left leg

Right foot steps backward

70%

30%

Right arm moves into Roll Back position

Left arm is in Ward-Off position

Waist turns to right

Right knee bends

Weight shifts onto right leg

20%

80%

2 Shift most of your weight onto the right leg, and turn your waist to the right. Lower the left arm toward the chest into the *Left Ward-Off* position (see p. 26) and begin to lower the right arm to thigh level.

Left hand curves inward

Waist turns farther to right

Left knee bends slightly

Weight increases on right leg

Left foot pivots to right on heel

15%

85%

3 Turn your waist farther to the right, and pivot on the left heel to an angle of 45 degrees to the right. Continue to lower the right arm until the hand is at thigh level in the *Roll Back* position (see p. 28).

PREVIOUS STAGES

Golden Rooster Stands on One Leg, p. 62 ———— Right Toe Kick, p. 64 ————

Right forearm rises

Waist turns to left

15%

85%

4 Turn your waist to the left, and raise the right arm across your body, with the palm facing to the left. As your waist turns, move the toes of both feet slightly to the left.

Right hand faces left

Left hand extends

Right forearm rises

6 Uncross the hands, and extend the right hand upward to shoulder height. Extend the left forearm forward, with the fingers outstretched and the palm facing to the right. Shifting all your weight onto the right leg, raise the left leg to shin height.

Right hand faces chest

Left wrist is under right wrist

Waist turns farther to left

15%

85%

5 Turn your waist farther to the left, and bend the left arm in toward your chest. Raise the right arm across your body until the wrist rests over the left wrist. Turn both palms in to face the chest.

Left leg rises

Left foot is relaxed

Left foot rises to shin height

Right knee bends to absorb weight

100%

轉身蹬腳 TURN BODY, HEEL KICK

This 180-degree turn can be difficult to perform, since a high level of stability is required. The sequence is aimed at developing and maintaining a strong root through the right foot while turning. Skilled practitioners of t'ai chi often execute this turn in one fluid, spinning movement, but beginners should keep the toes of the left foot touching the ground and tucked in behind the right foot for extra stability and control, pivoting on the right foot at their own speed as illustrated below. Both these methods of turning are considered equally acceptable.

Waist begins to turn to left

Toes of left foot touch ground

10%

90%

Waist turns to left

10%

90%

Waist turns farther to left

90%

10%

90%

10%

Waist continues to turn to left

Learning to turn
This composite photograph illustrates the actions in the first quarter-turn of the Turn Body sequence. For clarity, the movement is broken down into the four stages shown on the right (Steps One to Four).

1 Begin turning your waist slightly to the left, and place the toes of the left foot behind the right heel, with nearly all your weight on the right leg. Lower the arms to hip level, with the palms facing inward.

2 Keep turning your waist to the left, and pivot to the left on the right heel, moving the arms with the waist. Stablize through the toes of the left foot if you feel unstable.

3 Continue to pivot to the left on the right heel, with the weight still on the right leg and the arms moving with the waist.

4 Complete the first quarter-turn of the movement by pivoting farther on the right heel and turning your waist to the left.

PREVIOUS STAGES

Right Toe Kick, p. 64 ———— Left Toe Kick, p. 66 ————

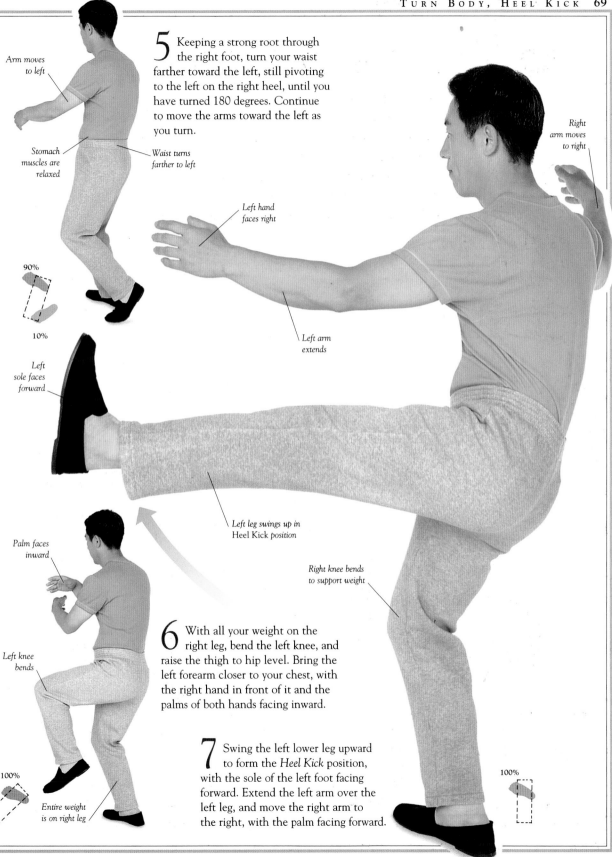

Arm moves to left

5 Keeping a strong root through the right foot, turn your waist farther toward the left, still pivoting to the left on the right heel, until you have turned 180 degrees. Continue to move the arms toward the left as you turn.

Right arm moves to right

Stomach muscles are relaxed

Waist turns farther to left

Left hand faces right

90%

10%

Left arm extends

Left sole faces forward

Palm faces inward

Left leg swings up in Heel Kick position

Right knee bends to support weight

6 With all your weight on the right leg, bend the left knee, and raise the thigh to hip level. Bring the left forearm closer to your chest, with the right hand in front of it and the palms of both hands facing inward.

Left knee bends

100%

Entire weight is on right leg

7 Swing the left lower leg upward to form the *Heel Kick* position, with the sole of the left foot facing forward. Extend the left arm over the left leg, and move the right arm to the right, with the palm facing forward.

100%

摟 膝 拗 步 BRUSH KNEE, TWIST STEP

Performed here for the second time in the form, *Brush Knee, Twist Step* differs from the first version (see p. 35) in that the action progresses from right to left rather than from left to right. The other major difference between the two sequences is that here, the movement is not broken up by *Strum the Lute* (see p. 36). Otherwise, the function of both is much the same, teaching how to coordinate the actions of the opposite pairs of arms and legs, and how to transfer the body weight smoothly from one leg to the other while moving forward.

Fingers of right hand align with ear

1 Relax the left leg from the knee so that it hangs loosely for a moment, with the toes pointing slightly downward. Lower the left arm to the inside of the left knee. Raise the right hand until the fingers are aligned with the right ear.

100%

Left foot lowers

2 With nearly all your weight on the right leg, place the left foot on the ground, putting the heel down first and rolling the rest of the foot onto the ground. Bend the right knee to absorb the weight.

Left foot lowers

Right knee bends

90%

10%

Left heel is placed down first

3 Shift your weight onto the left leg, bend the knee, and turn your waist slightly to the left. Leave the right hand behind the right ear. Begin to brush the left hand lightly past the top of the left knee.

Waist turns to left

Left knee bends

30%

70%

Weight shifts onto left leg

4 Transfer most of your weight onto the left leg, turn the waist farther to the left, and pivot on the right heel, turning the foot to the left. Move the right arm forward, and feel the energy flow between the left foot and the right palm.

Right arm extends forward

Waist turns farther to left

20%

80%

Right foot pivots on heel to left

PREVIOUS STAGES

Left Toe Kick, p. 66 ———— Turn Body, Heel Kick, p. 68

5 Shifting most of your weight onto the right leg, turn your waist to the left, and straighten the left leg as you go. Pivot the left foot slightly to the left so that the toes point to the left. Lower the right arm, bending the wrist, and pointing the fingers downward.

Waist turns to left

Left foot pivots slightly to left

80%

20%

6 With nearly all your weight on the right foot, turn your waist farther to the left. Pivot the left heel slightly farther to the left, and raise the left forearm, the palm curved forward. Raise the right forearm slightly.

Right forearm rises

Left arm moves with waist

Weight increases on right leg

90%

Left heel begins to pivot

10%

7 Shift most of your weight back onto the left leg, bending it to absorb your weight. Turn your waist to the right, and lower the right arm. Raise the left forearm from the elbow until the hand is level with the left ear.

Left hand is level with left ear

20%

Weight shifts onto left leg

80%

9 Shift most of your weight onto the right leg, and turn your waist to the right. Pivot the left foot on the heel to follow the waist. Extend the left arm with the palm facing forward until the fingers are at shoulder height; feel the energy flowing between the right *yung ch'uan* point (see p. 21), and the left palm, mirroring Step Four.

Fingers of left hand are at shoulder height

Right wrist twists slightly to right

Stomach muscles are relaxed

8 Increasing the weight on the left leg, step forward and to the right with the right foot, placing the heel down first before rolling down onto the rest of the foot. Lower the left forearm slightly so that the hand passes the left ear.

Left hand passes left ear

Weight shifts onto right leg

Right foot moves forward

10%

90%

Front of left foot turns slightly with turning waist

75%

25%

進步栽捶 STEP FORWARD, AND PLANT A PUNCH

Although this might appear to be an aggressive sequence if taken out of the context of t'ai chi practice, the punch must be carefully controlled. The movement here is forward, but it is also downward, building up energy for the final punch. The low stance for the punch counterbalances the high stances in *Brush Knee, Twist Step* (see p. 70), while the energy and power behind the punch are generated by the forward movement of the waist and upper body. The weight of the whole body, as opposed to just the arms, should move forward and sink into the punch.

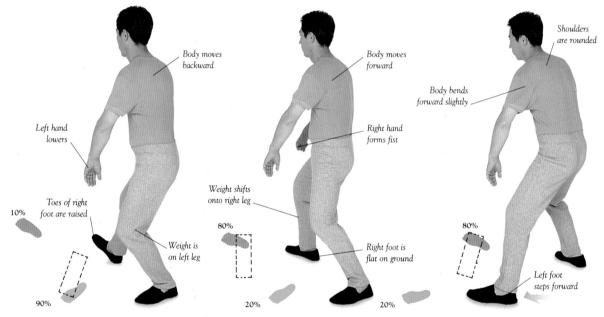

Body moves backward

Left hand lowers

Toes of right foot are raised

10%

90%

Weight is on left leg

Body moves forward

Right hand forms fist

Weight shifts onto right leg

80%

20%

Right foot is flat on ground

20%

Shoulders are rounded

Body bends forward slightly

80%

Left foot steps forward

1 Shift nearly all your weight onto the left leg, sink back, raise the toes of the right foot, and pivot the right heel to the right. Lower the left hand to thigh level, so that the fingers of both hands are pointing downward, and both palms are facing the thighs.

2 Transfer most of your weight onto the right leg, and roll the right foot down to the ground. Bend the right leg to absorb your weight as the body moves forward over the right leg. Form a relaxed fist with the right hand, with the knuckles facing forward.

3 With both knees bent slightly inward, take a step forward with the left foot so that the heel is level with the toes of the right foot. Round the shoulders, and bend forward from your waist so that both arms hang loosely in front of the thighs.

PREVIOUS STAGES

└ p. 69 ┘ └ **Brush Knee, Twist Step, p. 70** ┘

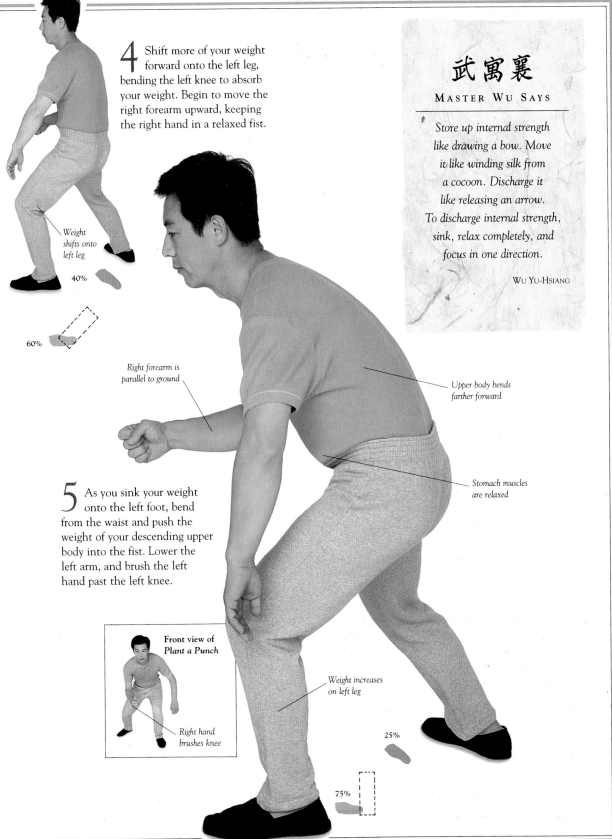

4 Shift more of your weight forward onto the left leg, bending the left knee to absorb your weight. Begin to move the right forearm upward, keeping the right hand in a relaxed fist.

武寓裏

MASTER WU SAYS

Store up internal strength like drawing a bow. Move it like winding silk from a cocoon. Discharge it like releasing an arrow. To discharge internal strength, sink, relax completely, and focus in one direction.

WU YU-HSIANG

Weight shifts onto left leg

40%

60%

Right forearm is parallel to ground

Upper body bends farther forward

Stomach muscles are relaxed

5 As you sink your weight onto the left foot, bend from the waist and push the weight of your descending upper body into the fist. Lower the left arm, and brush the left hand past the left knee.

Front view of Plant a Punch

Right hand brushes knee

Weight increases on left leg

25%

75%

進步右掤 STEP FORWARD TO RIGHT WARD-OFF

Although this final *Right Ward-Off* is similar to the first (see p. 27), an extra step is included at the beginning. This is necessary because the last stage of the previous sequence (see p. 73) requires a low stance, making the rising and stepping forward movement of this *Right Ward-Off* very powerful. It is important to keep the footwork in this sequence controlled and relaxed, but still full of energy and power; once this is mastered, it becomes easy to turn the waist correctly.

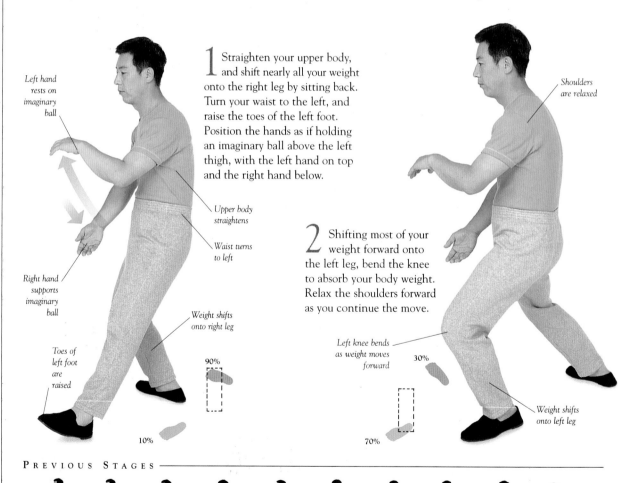

Left hand rests on imaginary ball

1 Straighten your upper body, and shift nearly all your weight onto the right leg by sitting back. Turn your waist to the left, and raise the toes of the left foot. Position the hands as if holding an imaginary ball above the left thigh, with the left hand on top and the right hand below.

Upper body straightens

Waist turns to left

Right hand supports imaginary ball

Weight shifts onto right leg

Toes of left foot are raised

90%

10%

Shoulders are relaxed

2 Shifting most of your weight forward onto the left leg, bend the knee to absorb your body weight. Relax the shoulders forward as you continue the move.

Left knee bends as weight moves forward

30%

Weight shifts onto left leg

70%

PREVIOUS STAGES

└─ **Brush Knee, Twist Step, p. 70** ─┘ └─ **Step Forward, and Plant a Punch**, p. 72 ─┘

"Feel the connection between the rooted foot, relaxed lower back, and the arm in Ward-Off"

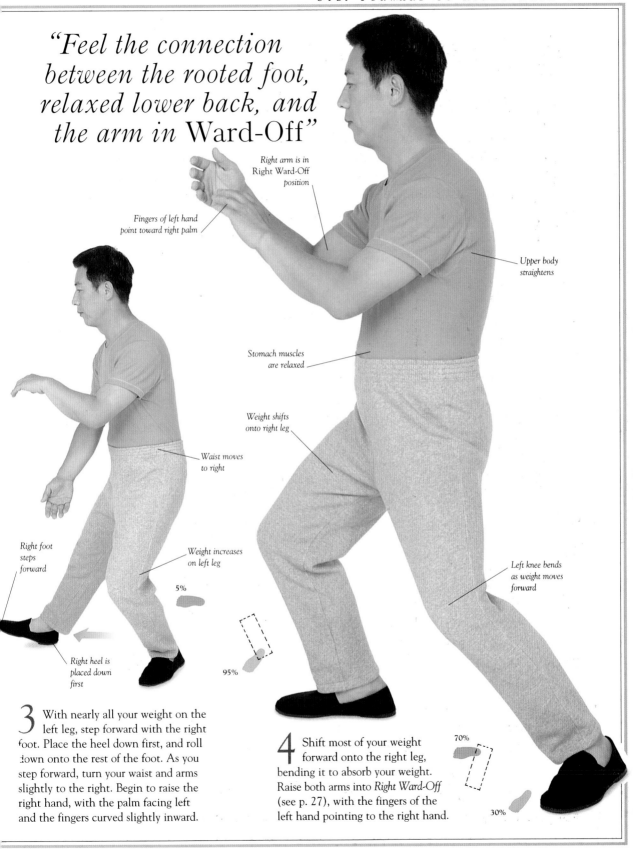

Right arm is in
Right Ward-Off
position

Fingers of left hand
point toward right palm

Upper body
straightens

Stomach muscles
are relaxed

Weight shifts
onto right leg

Waist moves
to right

Right foot
steps
forward

Weight increases
on left leg

5%

Left knee bends
as weight moves
forward

Right heel is
placed down
first

95%

3 With nearly all your weight on the left leg, step forward with the right foot. Place the heel down first, and roll down onto the rest of the foot. As you step forward, turn your waist and arms slightly to the right. Begin to raise the right hand, with the palm facing left and the fingers curved slightly inward.

4 Shift most of your weight forward onto the right leg, bending it to absorb your weight. Raise both arms into *Right Ward-Off* (see p. 27), with the fingers of the left hand pointing to the right hand.

70%

30%

攌 擠 按 ROLL BACK, PRESS, AND PUSH

Following on from *Right Ward-Off* for the third time in the form, this sequence of three distinct stances will now feel familiar. The movements of *Roll Back* are controlled by turning the waist and hip joints, and all the moves issue from the waist; the arms should never move independently of the waist and upper body. A strong root through the legs is vital, and a strong connection between the legs and the upper body is fundamental to developing *fa ching* energy (see p. 28) from the base of the spine.

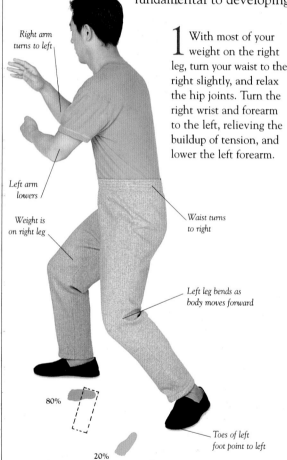

Right arm
turns to left

Left arm
lowers

Weight is
on right leg

Waist turns
to right

Left leg bends as
body moves forward

80%

20%

Toes of left
foot point to left

1 With most of your weight on the right leg, turn your waist to the right slightly, and relax the hip joints. Turn the right wrist and forearm to the left, relieving the buildup of tension, and lower the left forearm.

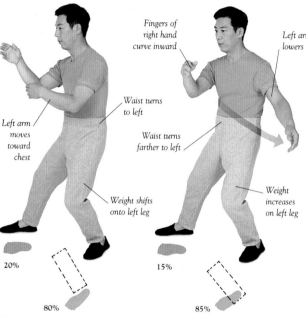

Fingers of
right hand
curve inward

Left arm
moves
toward
chest

Waist turns
to left

Weight shifts
onto left leg

20%

80%

Left arm
lowers

Waist turns
farther to left

Weight
increases
on left leg

15%

85%

2 Transfer most of your weight back onto the left leg, and begin to turn your waist to the left. Move the arms and upper body to the left at the same time, bringing the left arm slightly toward the front of the body.

3 Increasing the weight on the left leg, continue to turn your waist to the left. Curve the fingers of the right hand inward at chest height, and lower the left arm in a relaxed swinging motion out to the left of the thigh.

PREVIOUS STAGES

Step Forward, and Plant a Punch, p. 72 ——————

Step Forward to Right Ward-Off, p. 74

Hands are in ress position

Left arm rises

Waist turns to right

Weight shifts onto right leg

70%

30%

4 Transfer most of your weight onto the right leg, and turn your waist to the right. At the same time, bring the left arm across your body at chest height, and wrap the fingers of the left hand gently over the right hand, with the palms facing each other. Push the entire upper body forward into the *Press* position (see p. 29).

"Fa ching *energy is generated from a firmly rooted stance*"

Hands are in the Push position

Palm faces downward

Body moves forward

Fingers extend slightly

Upper body straightens

Weight shifts onto left leg

Left knee bends

Right knee bends

25%

75%

Weight shifts onto right leg

5 Shift most of your weight back onto the left leg. Uncross the hands, and extend the fingertips slightly upward and outward so that they are at shoulder height, bending the wrists slightly downward.

6 Transfer most of your weight onto the right leg, and bend it slightly to absorb the weight. Push the forearms, shoulders, and upper body forward all together into the *Push* position (see p. 29).

70%

30%

轉身掉手 TURN THE BODY, AND LOWER THE HANDS

This is the second use of *Turn the Body, and Lower the Hands* within the form. Here, as before, it follows *Roll Back, Press, and Push* (see p. 76) and precedes *Single Whip*. Comprising three steps, this sequence embodies several basic t'ai chi techniques: sitting back on the left leg and lowering the arms, which releases tension in the arms and shoulders; turning the waist, which enhances the ability to root through the weighted foot; and turning the waist while moving the arms in the same direction.

1 Shift most of your weight onto the left leg, and sink backward as you do so. Lower both forearms until they are parallel with the ground, relax the wrists, and extend the fingers downward slightly.

Forearm lowers

Fingers extend

Weight is on left leg

Right arm moves to left

20%

80%

2 Increasing the weight on the left leg, turn your waist to the left, and move both arms to the left at the same time. Pivot very slightly to the left on the right heel.

Toes of right foot move to left

15%

85%

Right hand rests on imaginary ball

Left hand supports imaginary ball

Waist turns to right

Waist turns to left

Weight shifts onto right leg

80%

20%

Weight increases on left leg

3 Transfer most of your weight onto the right leg, and turn your waist to the right. Position the arms as if holding an imaginary ball over the right thigh, with the right hand on top and the left hand below.

PREVIOUS STAGES

Step Forward to Right Ward-Off, p. 74

Roll Back, Press, and Push, p. 76

單鞭 SINGLE WHIP

In the third of four repetitions of *Single Whip* (see p. 31), the energy stored in the rooting of the legs and the relaxed, powerful turns of the waist is released in the expansive final position. These energies and movements can be applied to a range of situations in pushing hands and self-defense applications – the subtle shifting movements of the body, and the complex footwork, involved in this sequence make it possible to step out around an incoming threat, to deflect the energy of the attack.

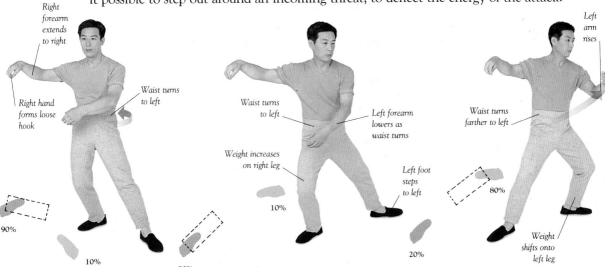

Right forearm extends to right

Right hand forms loose hook

Waist turns to left

90%

10%

90%

Waist turns to left

Left forearm lowers as waist turns

Weight increases on right leg

Left foot steps to left

10%

20%

Left arm rises

Waist turns farther to left

80%

Weight shifts onto left leg

1 Start to turn your waist to the left. Extend the right forearm to the right at shoulder height, relax the right wrist, and form a loose hook with the right hand. As you turn your waist toward the left, raise the left heel and turn the foot to the left.

2 With nearly all your weight on the right leg, turn your waist farther to the left, taking a step to the left and out with the left foot, so that it is just over one shoulders' width from the right foot. Lower the left forearm until it is level with the right thigh.

3 Start to shift your weight onto the left leg, turning your waist to the left, and bending the left knee to absorb the weight. Raise the left forearm across your body until the hand is at shoulder height, with the fingers curved inward toward the chest.

APPLICATION

Defender

Opponent

Right arm is pushed downward

To intercept an opponent's punch, the defender raises his arms into a relaxed *Single Whip*, taking hold of the opponent's right wrist with the right hand. Using the left palm to press the opponent's right shoulder downward, the defender immobilizes the opponent's right arm, and steps backward to the left. As pressure increases on the opponent's right shoulder, he is pushed forward and downward, and is finally immobilized.

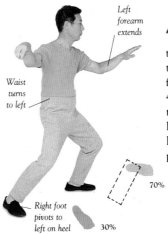

Left forearm extends

Waist turns to left

Right foot pivots to left on heel

70%

30%

4 Place more weight on the left leg, turning your waist farther to the left. Turn the right foot to the left, and pivot 45 degrees to the left on the right heel. Raise the left hand to shoulder level, with the palm pointing forward.

玉女穿梭 *FAIR LADY WORKS SHUTTLES I*

Many beginners regard this long sequence, which is illustrated over the following eight pages, as the most demanding part of the form. Its name derives from its similarity to the action of a woman using a traditional Chinese loom. This action is repeated in all four compass directions – here called the "four corners." The key to performing *Fair Lady Works Shuttles* is to shift the body weight at exactly the right moment to free up the legs, and to ensure that the hip joints relax as the weight shifts.

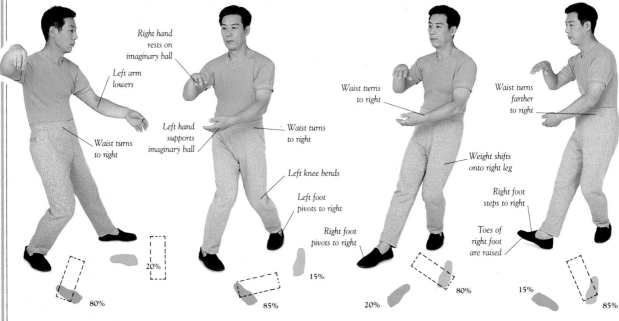

Right hand rests on imaginary ball

Left arm lowers

Waist turns to right

Left hand supports imaginary ball

Waist turns to right

Left knee bends

Left foot pivots to right

Right foot pivots to right

20%

80%

85%

15%

Waist turns to right

Waist turns farther to right

Weight shifts onto right leg

Right foot steps to right

Toes of right foot are raised

20%

80%

15%

85%

1 Shift most of your weight onto the right leg, and bend the right knee. Start to turn your waist to the right, and begin lowering the left arm, moving the forearm down and back up in front of your body to waist level.

2 Turn your waist farther around to the right, and pivot 90 degrees to the right on the left foot. Position both hands as if holding an imaginary ball above the right thigh, with the right hand on top and the left below.

3 Shifting most of your weight onto the left leg, relax the right hip joint to release the energy. Pivot 90 degrees to the right on the right foot, twisting on the ball of the foot until both feet face the same direction.

4 Transfer nearly all your weight onto the left leg, turn your waist to the right, and step to the right with the right foot. Place the right heel down in front of the left foot, with the toes pointing at a 90-degree angle to the right.

PREVIOUS STAGES

└ **Roll Back, Press, and Push,** p. 77 ┘ └ **Turn the Body, and Lower the Hands,** p. 78 ┘ └─── **Single Whip,** p. 79 ───

Shoulders
are relaxed

Right knee
bends

Weight shifts
onto right leg

Left forearm
rises

Left heel
rises

80%

10%

20%

Left wrist
turns to left

Right forearm
extends forward

Left foot
steps forward

5 Shift nearly all your weight back onto the right leg, bending the right knee to absorb your weight. Raise the left heel at the same time as your body moves forward, and make sure that the shoulders and hips are relaxed.

6 Step forward with the left foot, placing it at a 90-degree angle to the right foot. Raise the left forearm in front of your chest, with the left palm facing inward.

Waist turns
to left

Left palm
faces inward

Left forearm
rises

Right forearm
rises

Stomach muscles
are relaxed

Weight increases
on left leg

Right foot
pivots
to left

7 Transfer most of your weight onto the left leg, bend the leg to absorb your body weight, and sink down onto the left leg as you do so. Raise the left forearm, with the palm facing inward, and raise the right forearm to shoulder level.

8 Turn your waist to the left, pivoting the right foot 45 degrees to the left. Raise the left hand to forehead level, and turn the wrist so that the palm faces outward. Extend the right forearm at shoulder height so that you form the first corner of *Fair Lady Works Shuttles.*

30%

Weight
shifts onto
left leg

70%

25%

75%

FAIR LADY WORKS SHUTTLES II

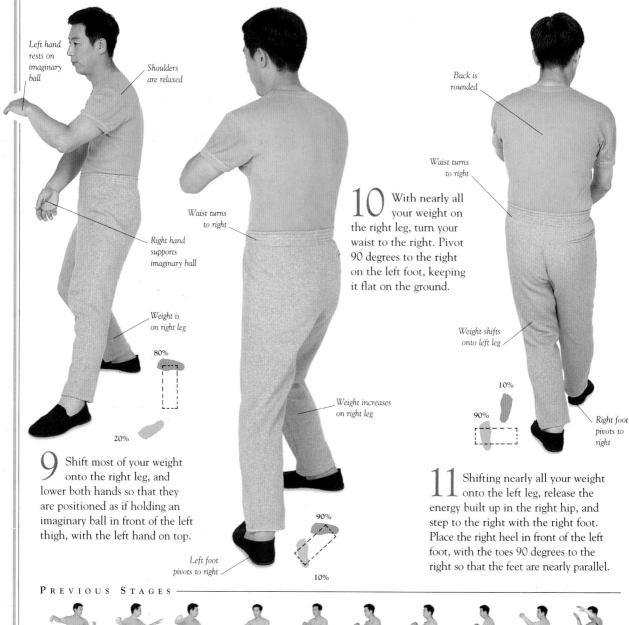

Left hand rests on imaginary ball

Shoulders are relaxed

Right hand supports imaginary ball

Waist turns to right

Weight is on right leg

80%

20%

9 Shift most of your weight onto the right leg, and lower both hands so that they are positioned as if holding an imaginary ball in front of the left thigh, with the left hand on top.

Waist turns to right

Weight increases on right leg

90%

10%

Left foot pivots to right

10 With nearly all your weight on the right leg, turn your waist to the right. Pivot 90 degrees to the right on the left foot, keeping it flat on the ground.

Back is rounded

Waist turns to right

Weight shifts onto left leg

10%

90%

Right foot pivots to right

11 Shifting nearly all your weight onto the left leg, release the energy built up in the right hip, and step to the right with the right foot. Place the right heel in front of the left foot, with the toes 90 degrees to the right so that the feet are nearly parallel.

PREVIOUS STAGES

Single Whip, p. 79   Fair Lady Works Shuttles I, p. 80

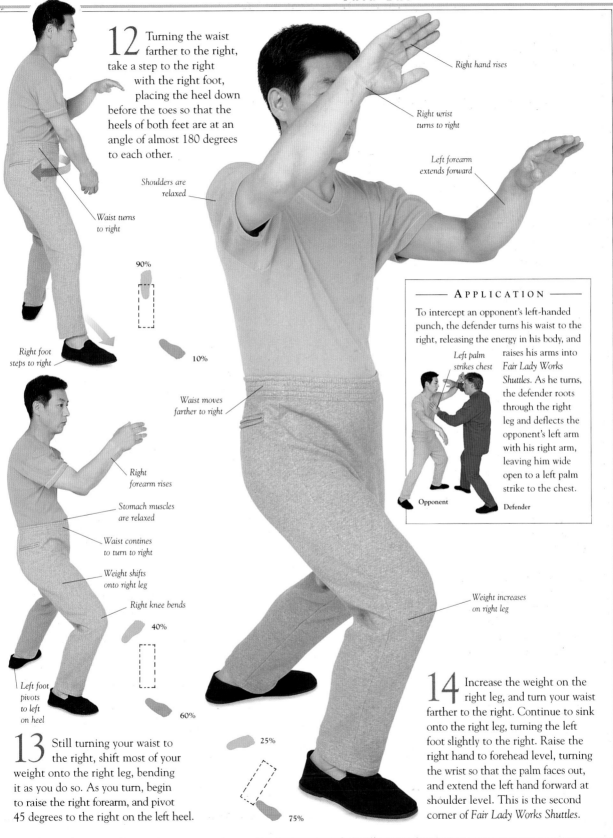

12 Turning the waist farther to the right, take a step to the right with the right foot, placing the heel down before the toes so that the heels of both feet are at an angle of almost 180 degrees to each other.

Right hand rises

Right wrist turns to right

Left forearm extends forward

Shoulders are relaxed

Waist turns to right

90%

10%

Right foot steps to right

Waist moves farther to right

Right forearm rises

Stomach muscles are relaxed

Waist contines to turn to right

Weight shifts onto right leg

Right knee bends

40%

Left foot pivots to left on heel

60%

Weight increases on right leg

25%

75%

APPLICATION

To intercept an opponent's left-handed punch, the defender turns his waist to the right, releasing the energy in his body, and raises his arms into *Fair Lady Works Shuttles*. As he turns, the defender roots through the right leg and deflects the opponent's left arm with his right arm, leaving him wide open to a left palm strike to the chest.

Left palm strikes chest

Opponent

Defender

13 Still turning your waist to the right, shift most of your weight onto the right leg, bending it as you do so. As you turn, begin to raise the right forearm, and pivot 45 degrees to the right on the left heel.

14 Increase the weight on the right leg, and turn your waist farther to the right. Continue to sink onto the right leg, turning the left foot slightly to the right. Raise the right hand to forehead level, turning the wrist so that the palm faces out, and extend the left hand forward at shoulder level. This is the second corner of *Fair Lady Works Shuttles*.

FAIR LADY WORKS SHUTTLES *III*

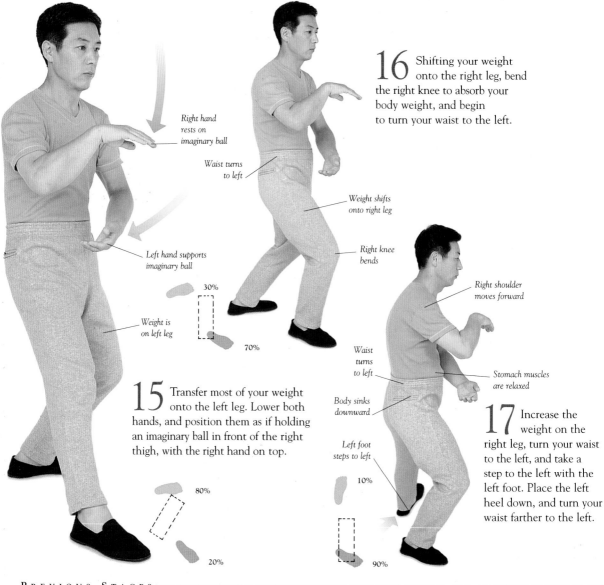

Right hand rests on imaginary ball

Waist turns to left

16 Shifting your weight onto the right leg, bend the right knee to absorb your body weight, and begin to turn your waist to the left.

Weight shifts onto right leg

Left hand supports imaginary ball

Right knee bends

Weight is on left leg

30%

70%

15 Transfer most of your weight onto the left leg. Lower both hands, and position them as if holding an imaginary ball in front of the right thigh, with the right hand on top.

Right shoulder moves forward

Waist turns to left

Stomach muscles are relaxed

Body sinks downward

Left foot steps to left

10%

17 Increase the weight on the right leg, turn your waist to the left, and take a step to the left with the left foot. Place the left heel down, and turn your waist farther to the left.

80%

20%

90%

PREVIOUS STAGES

Fair Lady Works Shuttles I, p. 80 ———— Fair Lady Works Shuttles II, p. 82 ————

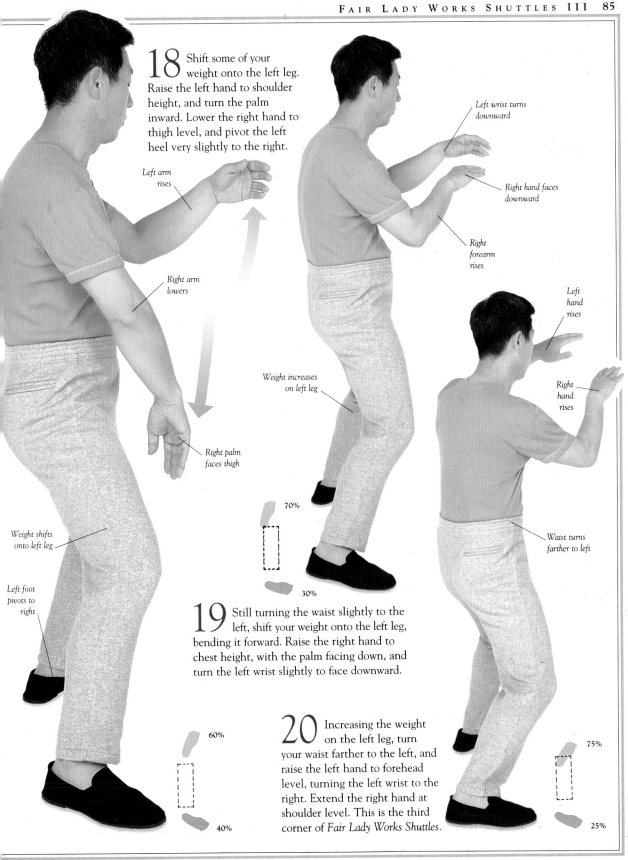

18 Shift some of your weight onto the left leg. Raise the left hand to shoulder height, and turn the palm inward. Lower the right hand to thigh level, and pivot the left heel very slightly to the right.

Left arm rises

Right arm lowers

Right palm faces thigh

Weight shifts onto left leg

Left foot pivots to right

Left wrist turns downward

Right hand faces downward

Right forearm rises

Weight increases on left leg

70%

30%

19 Still turning the waist slightly to the left, shift your weight onto the left leg, bending it forward. Raise the right hand to chest height, with the palm facing down, and turn the left wrist slightly to face downward.

60%

40%

Left hand rises

Right hand rises

Waist turns farther to left

20 Increasing the weight on the left leg, turn your waist farther to the left, and raise the left hand to forehead level, turning the left wrist to the right. Extend the right hand at shoulder level. This is the third corner of *Fair Lady Works Shuttles*.

75%

25%

FAIR LADY WORKS SHUTTLES *IV*

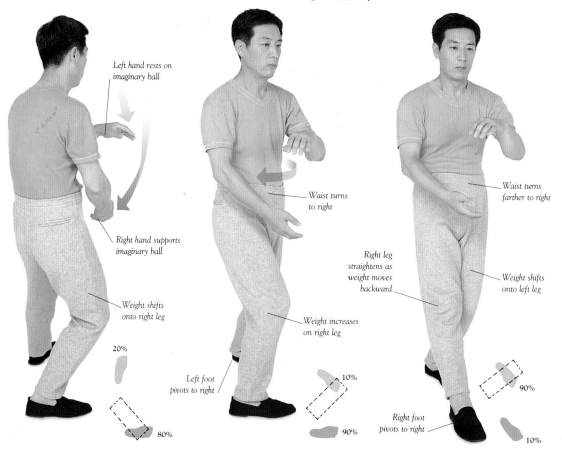

Left hand rests on imaginary ball

Right hand supports imaginary ball

Weight shifts onto right leg

20%

80%

Waist turns to right

Left foot pivots to right

Weight increases on right leg

10%

90%

Waist turns farther to right

Weight shifts onto left leg

Right leg straightens as weight moves backward

Right foot pivots to right

90%

10%

21 Shift most of your weight onto the right leg, straightening the left leg slightly as you move your weight backward. Lower both arms, and position the hands as if holding an imaginary ball above the right thigh, with the left hand on top and the right hand supporting below.

22 Increasing the weight on the right leg, begin to turn your waist around to the right. Keeping the left foot placed flat on the ground, pivot it so that it moves to an angle of 90 degrees to the right, until the toes of the left foot are pointing toward the toes of the right foot.

23 Shift nearly all your weight backward onto the left leg, straightening the right leg, and continue to turn your waist farther around to the right. Pivot on the ball of the right foot to an angle of 45 degrees to the right, until both feet point in the same direction.

PREVIOUS STAGES

Fair Lady Works Shuttles II, p. 82   **Fair Lady Works Shuttles III, p. 84**

"To sink comfortably into each of the four corners, the body must be relaxed"

24 Take a step to the right with the right foot so that the heels are positioned at an angle of almost 180 degrees to each other. Place the right heel down first, and continue to turn your waist to the right.

Stomach muscles are relaxed

Waist turns to right

Right hand turns counterclockwise

Right arm rises

Right forearm rises

Waist moves farther to right

Right [fo]ot steps to right

Weight shifts onto left leg

Waist turns to right

Weight increases on right leg

Left foot pivots to right on heel

10%

90%

75%

25%

Weight shifts onto right leg

60%

40%

Left heel pivots to right

25 Still turning your waist to the right, shift more of your weight onto the right leg. As you turn, raise the right forearm, and pivot on the left foot 90 degrees toward the right.

26 Turn your waist farther to the right, and sink onto the right leg. Pivot 45 degrees to the right on the left heel, raise the right hand to forehead level, and the left hand to shoulder level, in the final corner of *Fair Lady Works Shuttles*.

左掤 *LEFT WARD-OFF*

As the previous occurrences have taught, *Left Ward-Off* is governed by the movements of the waist and legs, combined with a relaxed, fluid feeling in the upper body. The sequence helps to improve rooting skills; each time the weight is shifted from one leg to the other, the foot should feel as though it is being screwed into the ground. This creates a strong root, which in turn produces a vast amount of energy in the legs and lower back. Subsequently, this energy is released to power the next move.

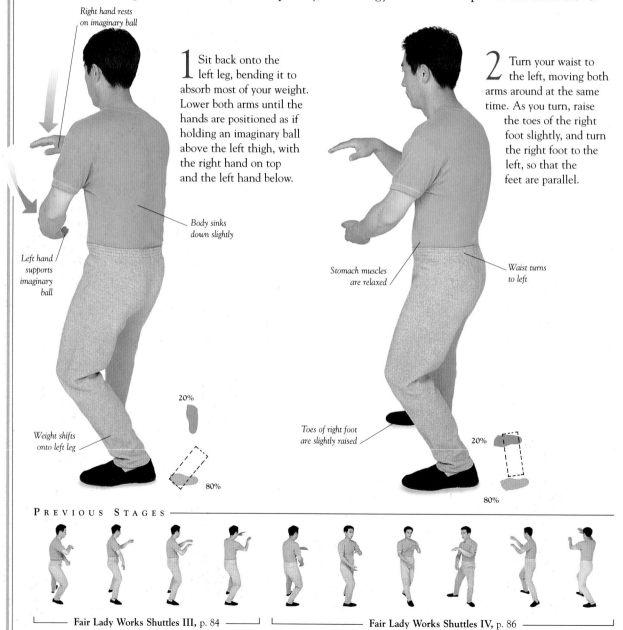

Right hand rests on imaginary ball

1 Sit back onto the left leg, bending it to absorb most of your weight. Lower both arms until the hands are positioned as if holding an imaginary ball above the left thigh, with the right hand on top and the left hand below.

Body sinks down slightly

Left hand supports imaginary ball

Weight shifts onto left leg

20%

80%

2 Turn your waist to the left, moving both arms around at the same time. As you turn, raise the toes of the right foot slightly, and turn the right foot to the left, so that the feet are parallel.

Stomach muscles are relaxed

Waist turns to left

Toes of right foot are slightly raised

20%

80%

PREVIOUS STAGES

Fair Lady Works Shuttles III, p. 84 ———— Fair Lady Works Shuttles IV, p. 86

3 Continuing to turn the waist to the left, shift most of your weight onto the right leg, relieving the pressure on the left hip. Step out and to the left with the left foot, and place the heel down first.

Waist turns to left

Weight shifts onto right leg

95%

5%

Left foot steps out and to left

4 Continue to turn your waist to the left, slowly transferring your weight onto the left leg as you do so. Lower the right forearm to thigh level, and raise the left arm to chest height, with the palm held just above the right wrist.

Right arm lowers

Left arm rises

Waist turns farther to left

Weight shifts onto left leg

40%

60%

Body faces forward

Left arm is in Ward-Off position

Right forearm lowers

Right hand faces backward

5 Increasing the weight on the left leg, turn your waist to the left until you face forward. Pivot the right foot to an angle of 45 degrees to the left, raise the left arm to chest height, and sink down into the *Left Ward-Off* position (see p. 26).

Weight increases on left leg

30%

70%

Right foot pivots to left

APPLICATION

To intercept a right-handed punch from an opponent, the defender raises his left arms into *Lift Hands* (see p. 32) before shifting his weight on to the left leg and forming *Left Ward-Off*. Seizing the opponent's right wrist with his right hand, he immobilizes the opponent's right arm, by straightening the arm and locking his elbow joint. The pressure on his elbow, ribs, and right knee will force the opponent to abandon his attack.

Arm is in Ward-off position

Defender

Opponent

RIGHT WARD-OFF, ROLL BACK, PRESS, AND PUSH

右
掤
搌
擠
按

Performed here for the fourth time in the form, these postures should now feel familiar. The difference between form and application can now be appreciated. In the form, it is vital to adhere to the postures illustrated; in application (see p. 114) it is necessary to adapt, improvise around, and expand upon the basic positions, energies, and forces of the form. These are the basics for developing t'ai chi further.

Left hand rests on imaginary ball

Right hand supports imaginary ball

Waist turns slightly to left

Weight is on left leg

Right foot steps to right

20%

80%

Waist turns to right

Weight increases on left leg

Right heel is placed down first

10%

90%

Arms extend in front of chest

Waist turns farther to right

Left foot pivots to right on heel

Weight shifts onto right leg

70%

30%

1 With most of your weight on the left leg, turn your waist slightly to the left. Place the hands as if holding an imaginary ball above the left thigh, with the left hand on top.

2 Turn your waist to the right, and move both arms around at the same time. Take a small step forward and slightly to the right with the right foot, placing the heel down first.

3 Shift your weight onto the right leg, and turn your waist farther to the right. Turn the left foot 45 degrees to the right, and raise both arms, sinking into the *Right Ward-Off* position (see p. 27).

PREVIOUS STAGES

Fair Lady Works Shuttles IV, p. 86 ——— **Left Ward-Off,** p. 88

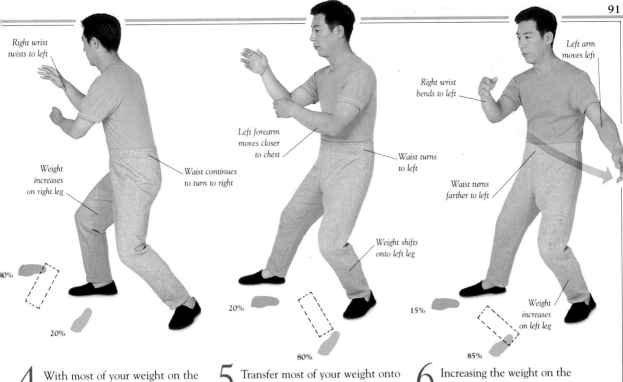

Right wrist twists to left

Weight increases on right leg

Waist continues to turn to right

0%

20%

Left forearm moves closer to chest

Waist turns to left

Weight shifts onto left leg

20%

80%

Left arm moves left

Right wrist bends to left

Waist turns farther to left

Weight increases on left leg

15%

85%

4 With most of your weight on the right leg, turn your waist farther to the right. Relax the right hip joint, and twist the right wrist slightly to the left, relieving tension in the arm.

5 Transfer most of your weight onto the left leg, and turn your waist to the left. As your weight transfers, sit back on the right leg, and move both arms to the left at the same time.

6 Increasing the weight on the left leg, turn your waist farther toward the left. Lower the left arm across your body until it is level with the right thigh.

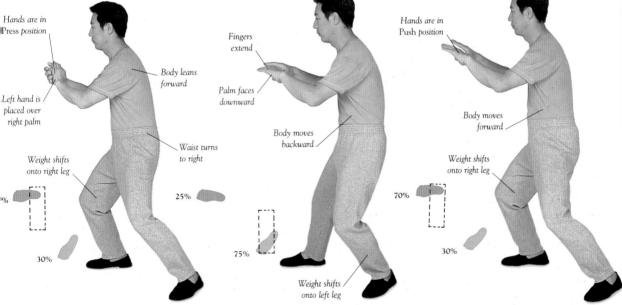

Hands are in Press position

Left hand is placed over right palm

Weight shifts onto right leg

Body leans forward

Waist turns to right

%

25%

30%

Fingers extend

Palm faces downward

Body moves backward

75%

Weight shifts onto left leg

Hands are in Push position

Body moves forward

Weight shifts onto right leg

70%

30%

7 Transfer most of your weight onto the right leg, and turn your waist to the right. Raise the left arm so that the arms are in the *Press* position (see p. 29), with the left hand over the right palm.

8 Shift most of your weight onto the left leg, and separate the hands slightly. Extend the fingers forward at shoulder height, and turn the right palm so that both palms face downward.

9 Move most of your weight back onto the right leg, bending the knee forward to absorb your weight. Extend the arms and body forward into the *Push* position (see p. 29).

轉身掉手 TURN THE BODY, AND LOWER THE HANDS

This is the third and final use of *Turn the Body, and Lower the Hands* in the form. As before, it follows on from the *Push* position (see p. 91) and stores up energy that is subsequently released in the following sequence. This is achieved by turning the waist to the left, and screwing the weighted foot into the ground to produce kinetic energy, which is important in the production of stability and power. There are two possible elbow strikes inherent in the turning of the waist, and these can be used to good effect against an opponent in application practice (see p. 116).

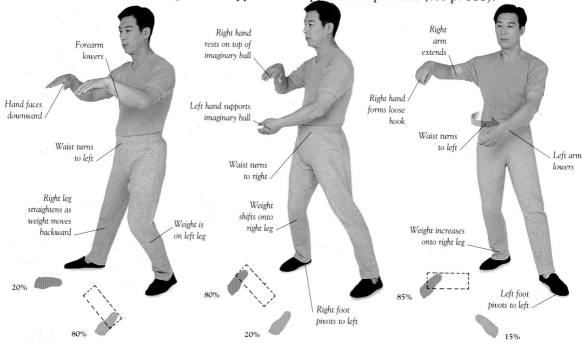

Forearm lowers

Right hand rests on top of imaginary ball

Right arm extends

Hand faces downward

Left hand supports imaginary ball

Right hand forms loose hook

Waist turns to left

Waist turns to right

Waist turns to left

Left arm lowers

Right leg straightens as weight moves backward

Weight is on left leg

Weight shifts onto right leg

Weight increases onto right leg

20%

80%

80%

20%

85%

Right foot pivots to left

Left foot pivots to left

15%

1 Start turning your waist to the left, and shift most of your weight onto the left leg. Lower both forearms to chest height, with the palms facing the floor and the fingers extended downward.

2 Pivot the right foot to the left, placing the hands as if holding an imaginary ball above the left thigh. Shift your weight onto the right leg, moving the arms as the waist turns to the right.

3 Turn your waist back to the left, increasing the weight on the right leg slightly. Pivot 90 degrees to the left on the ball of the left foot, and extend the right hand in a loose hook.

PREVIOUS STAGES

單鞭下勢

DESCENDING SINGLE WHIP I

Illustrated over the following three pages, this is the second example of *Descending Single Whip* and requires the same lowering of the stance in the final stages (see p. 61). Successful execution of the controlled, sinking movement in *Descending Single Whip* calls for strength and balance, and the emphasis should be on sinking as low as is stable and comfortable, not so far that the stance becomes unstable. The sunken stance generates energy to power the upward movement of the next sequence.

1 Taking a wide step to the left with the left foot, turn your waist slightly to the left, using some of the energy stored in the right leg. Move both arms to the left as you turn your waist.

Waist turns to left

Weight shifts onto left leg

80%

20%

2 Shift most of your weight onto the left leg, bending the knee slightly to absorb the weight as you move. At the same time, turn your waist to the left.

Waist turns slightly to left

Arm moves to left with waist

3 Continue to turn your waist to the left, moving both arms around simultaneously. Pivot to the left on the right heel, and raise the left forearm until the hand is at shoulder height, with the palm facing right and the fingers pointing upward.

Left forearm rises

Waist turns to left

Toes of right foot move to left

85%

15%

20%

Left foot steps to left

80%

DESCENDING SINGLE WHIP II

Right hand is in loose hook

4 Continue turning your waist to the left, and pivot 45 degrees to the left on the right heel. Extend the left forearm forward, twisting the wrist around to the left slightly, until the palm faces forward.

Left palm faces forward

Left forearm extends

Head follows movement of waist

Waist turns to left

5 Increasing the weight on the left leg, turn your body farther to the left. Pivot 45 degrees to the right on the right heel, so that the heels are at an angle of almost 180 degrees to each other.

Waist turns farther to left

Weight is on left leg

Right foot pivots to right on heel

Weight increases on left leg

Right heel pivots to left

70%

30%

85%

15%

PREVIOUS STAGES

└─── **Press, and Push,** p. 91 ───┘ └─── **Turn the Body,** p. 92 ───┘ └─── **Descending Single Whip I,** p. 93 ─┘

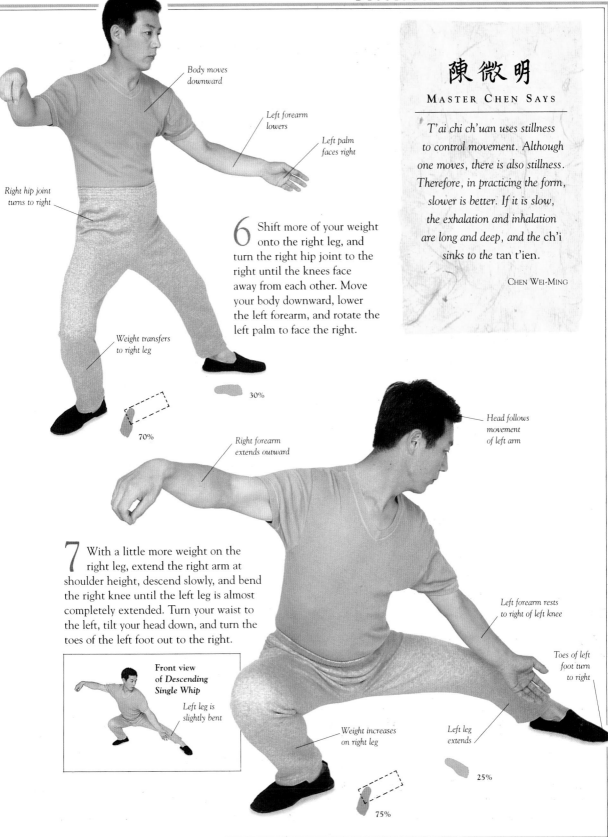

Body moves
downward

Left forearm
lowers

Left palm
faces right

Right hip joint
turns to right

6 Shift more of your weight
onto the right leg, and
turn the right hip joint to the
right until the knees face
away from each other. Move
your body downward, lower
the left forearm, and rotate the
left palm to face the right.

陳微明

MASTER CHEN SAYS

*T'ai chi ch'uan uses stillness
to control movement. Although
one moves, there is also stillness.
Therefore, in practicing the form,
slower is better. If it is slow,
the exhalation and inhalation
are long and deep, and the ch'i
sinks to the tan t'ien.*

CHEN WEI-MING

Weight transfers
to right leg

30%

70%

Right forearm
extends outward

Head follows
movement
of left arm

7 With a little more weight on the
right leg, extend the right arm at
shoulder height, descend slowly, and bend
the right knee until the left leg is almost
completely extended. Turn your waist to
the left, tilt your head down, and turn the
toes of the left foot out to the right.

Front view
of *Descending
Single Whip*

Left leg is
slightly bent

Left forearm rests
to right of left knee

Toes of left
foot turn
to right

Weight increases
on right leg

Left leg
extends

25%

75%

上步七星 STEP UP TO SEVEN STARS

At the beginning of *Step Up to Seven Stars*, the body rises from the low stance in the final stages of *Descending Single Whip* (see p. 95) by shifting the root smoothly from the right leg down through the left leg, and stepping forward with the right foot, keeping the body relaxed. It is the root that provides a stable base from which to step forward without losing stability. The final arm stance (Step Three) can be used in application as a strong, block-and-strike combination against an opponent.

Right arm lowers

Body rises

Left arm rises

Weight shifts onto left leg

Right foot steps forward

Right foot pivots to left on heel

60%

40%

Left arm rises

Left hand faces downward

Right arm moves forward

Weight increases on left leg

80%

20%

Toes of right foot touch ground first

Hands form relaxed fists

3 Increase the weight on the left leg, and step forward with the right foot, placing the heel down first. Raise the right arm to chest height, resting the wrist just below the left wrist. Form both hands into relaxed fists.

90%

10%

Right foot steps forward

1 Rise, and shift more of your weight onto the left leg. Pivot 45 degrees to the left on the right heel, and relax the right hand, lowering it to thigh level. Raise the left arm to chest height.

2 Take a step forward and in with the right foot, placing the toes down briefly for stability. Raise the left arm to chest height, turn the wrist so that the palm faces down, and move the right arm forward.

TESTING STEP 3

Instructor

To test the strength of the root down the left leg in *Seven Stars*, the instructor applies an even pressure to the student's elbows. Relaxing his shoulders, the student yields with the pressure, channeling it down through his arms, body, and left leg to the ground. At the same time, he keeps his stance firm.

Weight is rooted through left leg

Student

PREVIOUS STAGES

Turn the Body, p. 92 ─── Descending Single Whip I and II, p. 93, p. 94

退
步
跨
虎

STEP BACK TO RIDE THE TIGER

Similar in feel to *Step Back to Repulse the Monkey* (see p. 50), this sequence offers another chance to step backward, gathering strength and energy, before moving forward again. The two turns from the waist allow the body to move away from an attack, and the weight to shift from one leg to another without the feet moving. This provides the momentum for a right-handed strike in the final step, when the turn of the waist to the left is coordinated with the rise of the right arm.

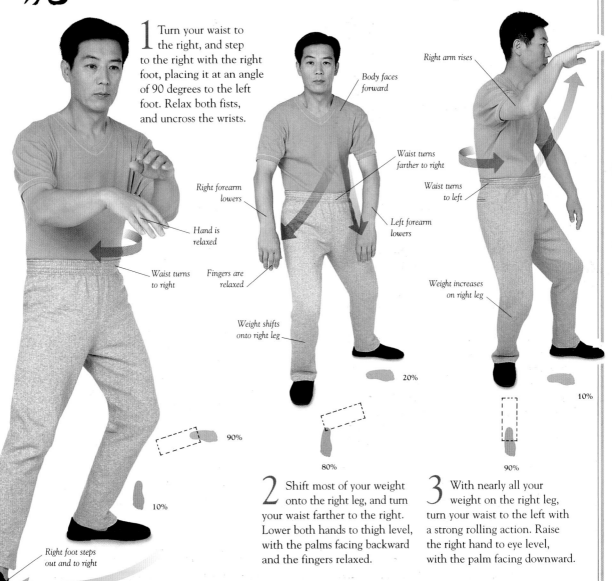

1 Turn your waist to the right, and step to the right with the right foot, placing it at an angle of 90 degrees to the left foot. Relax both fists, and uncross the wrists.

Right forearm lowers

Hand is relaxed

Waist turns to right

Fingers are relaxed

Right foot steps out and to right

10%

90%

Body faces forward

Waist turns farther to right

Left forearm lowers

Weight shifts onto right leg

20%

80%

2 Shift most of your weight onto the right leg, and turn your waist farther to the right. Lower both hands to thigh level, with the palms facing backward and the fingers relaxed.

Right arm rises

Waist turns to left

Weight increases on right leg

10%

90%

3 With nearly all your weight on the right leg, turn your waist to the left with a strong rolling action. Raise the right hand to eye level, with the palm facing downward.

轉身擺蓮腿

TURN BODY, LOTUS KICK

This is a difficult sequence, combining a complete turn with a high kick, and requiring great stability and accurate body alignment. In order to generate enough power in the waist to perform the kick successfully, the pivoting steps of the turn must be coordinated. Although when practicing the form it is vital to follow the sequences precisely, half a turn and a lower kick may be more effective in application, illustrating the point that the movements contained in the form are a basis for developing training techniques farther. In application (see p. 114) the basic moves are adapted to circumstance.

Making a fluid turn
This composite picture illustrates the first half of the Turn Body sequence, which is a 180-degree turn to the right. For clarity, the movement is broken down into the four stages shown on the right (Steps One to Four).

Waist turns slightly to left

Weight is on right leg

Right arm lowers

10%

90%

1 With most of your weight on the right leg, turn your waist to the left. Lower the right arm to thigh level and move the arms with the waist.

Waist turns to right

2 Turning your waist and arms to the right, shift your weight onto the right foot. Pivot to the right on the ball of the left foot.

Arm extends at chest height

Waist turns farther to right

5%

95%

Left leg rises slightly

5%

95%

3 Turn your waist farther to the right, and, with nearly all your weight on the right leg, raise the left leg. Extend the arms at chest height.

Left leg moves in front of right leg

5%

95%

Waist turns farther to right

4 Still turning the waist to the right, place the left leg in front of the right leg so that the feet form a right angle.

PREVIOUS STAGES

Descending Single Whip II, p. 94 — Step Up to Seven Stars, p. 96 — Ride the Tiger, p. 97

5 Continue to circle the left leg around to the right, pivoting on the ball of the right foot, and turn your waist a further 90 degrees to the right. Start to shift your weight onto the left leg.

Waist moves to right

10%

90%

6 Shift nearly all your weight onto the left leg, and continue to turn to the right, pivoting on the ball of the right foot. As you turn to the right, rotate the right foot until it is in front of the left foot.

Waist moves farther to right

Right foot turns to right

95%

5%

"When turning, root through the ball of the weighted foot"

Body bends forward

Right knee rises

Weight is on left leg

Right foot rises to waist height

8 Raise the right foot to waist height, keeping the knee slightly bent. Bend your body forward so that the fingers of both hands reach toward the toes of the right foot. Move the right leg to the left, brushing the toes of the right foot across the fingertips of the left hand, and then the fingertips of the right hand.

Toes of right foot brush fingers of both hands

100%

100%

7 With all your weight on the left leg, root down firmly, and bend the right knee, raising the right thigh to hip level. Align your lower back over the left foot, and relax the right foot.

APPLICATION

To avoid a right-handed punch from an opponent, the defender steps to the left, roots through the left leg, and relaxes. Kicking the right foot out at knee height in *Lotus Kick*, the defender contacts the side of the opponent's leg and uses the right hand to control the opponent's right arm.

Opponent   Defender

Left leg is stable

彎弓射虎

DRAW A BOW TO SHOOT THE TIGER

The power unleashed in this sequence is generated by using the weight of the whole body, not just that of the arms and shoulders. The key to developing this power lies in creating a strong root down through the right leg by coordinating the step forward with a rolling action of the waist. The moves are performed with the upper body and arms relaxed, which eases any tension that may have developed when performing the difficult spinning turn and slow kick of the previous sequence.

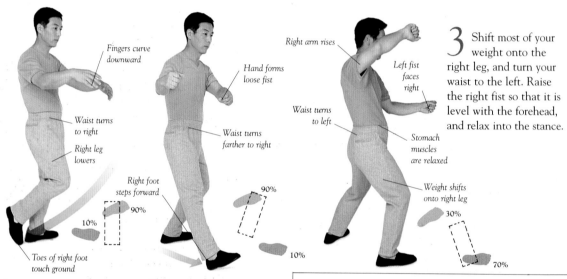

Fingers curve downward

Waist turns to right

Right leg lowers

Toes of right foot touch ground

10%

90%

Hand forms loose fist

Waist turns farther to right

Right foot steps forward

90%

10%

Right arm rises

Left fist faces right

Waist turns to left

Stomach muscles are relaxed

Weight shifts onto right leg

30%

70%

3 Shift most of your weight onto the right leg, and turn your waist to the left. Raise the right fist so that it is level with the forehead, and relax into the stance.

1 Lower the right leg, and rest the toes of the right foot on the ground, rooting briefly through the right foot. Turn your waist toward the right, and relax the arms, with the fingers curved downward. Turn both hands inward so that the palms face each other.

2 Take a step forward with the right foot, placing the heel down first, and then rolling down onto the rest of the foot. Turn your waist farther to the right, and move both arms to the right in a long, sweeping motion, forming loose fists with both hands.

APPLICATION

To intercept an opponent's left punch, the defender turns the waist to the right, following through with a powerful strike with the right fist to the opponent's jaw. Turning to the right into *Draw a Bow to Shoot the Tiger*, the defender follows through with a sharp jab to the opponent's stomach with the left fist.

Opponent *Defender*

Left hand forms fist

PREVIOUS STAGES

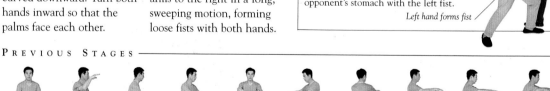

p. 97

Turn Body, Lotus Kick, p. 98

STEP FORWARD, MOVE, PARRY, AND PUNCH

進步搬攔捶

Appearing for the second time in the form, *Step Forward, Move, Parry, and Punch* is made up of four distinct stances, which have been individually incorporated into other sequences throughout the form. It is a difficult sequence to perform precisely, since the upper body and limbs need to be relaxed and moving smoothly as a single unit with the turning waist, to increase their power. The body must move naturally from side to side with the waist to settle into the flowing actions required.

1 Take a small step inward with the left foot, and turn your waist to the right. Lower the right arm to shoulder height, loosen both fists, and extend the fingers of the right hand.

Right hand lowers

Waist turns to right

Weight increases on right leg

Left foot steps inward

10%

90%

Right arm lowers

Left hand rises

Waist turns to right

Right hand forms loose fist

90%

10%

Right foot steps forward

2 Shift most of your weight onto the left leg, and turn farther to the right. Step forward with the right foot, and place the heel down first. Form a loose fist with the right hand, and lower it to hip level. Raise the left hand to shoulder height.

Left hand lowers

Left foot steps forward

Right fist turns to right

Weight shifts onto right leg

Weight shifts onto left leg

3 Shift nearly all your weight onto the right leg, and step forward with the left foot, placing the heel down first. Pivot on the right heel to the right. Twist the right fist to the right, and lower the left hand to chest height.

10%

90%

4 Transfer your weight forward onto the left leg, and roll the rest of your foot down onto the ground as you do so.

Weight shifts onto left leg

Left knee bends

60%

40%

Waist turns to left

Right heel pivots to left

5 Turn your waist toward the left, pivoting the right foot 45 degrees to the left. Move the arms into the *Punch* position (see p. 39).

Left palm supports right elbow

70%

30%

如封似閉 *APPARENT CLOSE-UP*

This is a repetition of an earlier sequence (p. 40), and in both instances *Apparent Close-Up* precedes *Cross Hands*. There is an apparent retreat in Step Two, but this becomes an attacking stance in Step Three, when the arms are extended at chest height into the *Push* position. The sequence involves shifting the weight from the front to the back leg, then to the front again, and is an exercise in moving the body from the waist without moving the feet. This technique is important in developing the skills required in pushing hands (see p. 108) and is used in applications (see p. 114).

Right forearm is extended

Left palm faces right elbow

Weight increases on right leg

60%

40%

Right fist loosens

Left palm faces to right

Right wrist crosses over left wrist

Body moves forward

40%

60%

Arms are in Push position

Waist turns to right

Weight shifts onto left leg

Weight shifts onto right leg

70%

30%

Forearm lowers to chest height

Body sinks slightly

Left foot turns to right

20%

80%

1 Continue to shift your weight onto the right leg, and lower the left hand until it is placed just under the right elbow, palm facing upward.

2 Increase the weight on the right leg, and loosen the right fist. Move the right arm inward, crossing the left forearm under the right wrist.

3 Shift some of your weight onto the left leg, and uncross the arms. Extend both arms forward in the *Push* position (see p. 29).

4 Transfer your weight onto the right leg, and turn your waist to the right. Turn the left foot to the right, and lower the forearms.

PREVIOUS STAGES

└── Lotus Kick, p. 99 ──┘   └── Shoot the Tiger, p. 100 ──┘   └── Step Forward, Move, Parry, and Punch, p. 101 ──┘

十字手 CROSS HANDS

Appearing here for the second time in the form (see p. 41), this sequence of *Cross Hands* gives another opportunity to practice adjusting the posture of the upper body without losing stability, or giving too much ground to an opponent in application. This is one of the rare occasions in t'ai chi when the body weight is evenly distributed through both legs. However, this only happens briefly, and the move is immediately superseded by a shift of weight and root to the left leg at the start of *Close T'ai Chi*, which is the final sequence of the Cheng Man-Ch'ing form.

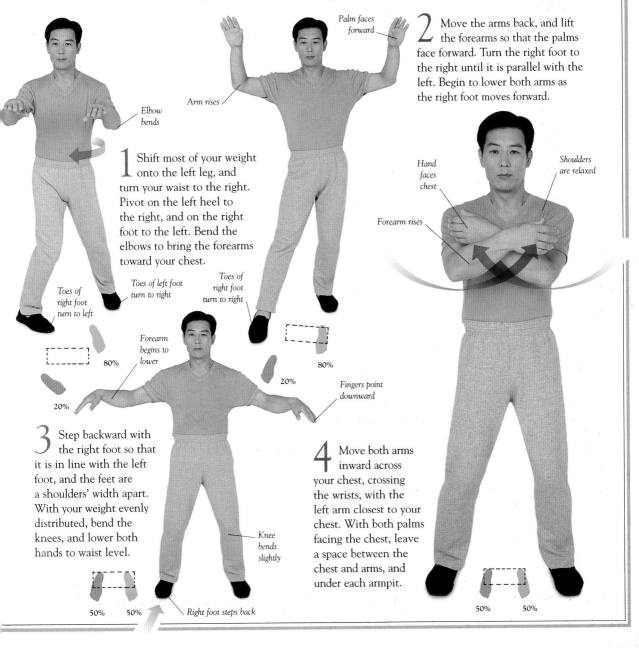

Palm faces forward

Arm rises

Elbow bends

2 Move the arms back, and lift the forearms so that the palms face forward. Turn the right foot to the right until it is parallel with the left. Begin to lower both arms as the right foot moves forward.

Hand faces chest

Shoulders are relaxed

Forearm rises

1 Shift most of your weight onto the left leg, and turn your waist to the right. Pivot on the left heel to the right, and on the right foot to the left. Bend the elbows to bring the forearms toward your chest.

Toes of left foot turn to right

Toes of right foot turn to right

Toes of right foot turn to left

80%

Forearm begins to lower

80%

20%

Fingers point downward

20%

3 Step backward with the right foot so that it is in line with the left foot, and the feet are a shoulders' width apart. With your weight evenly distributed, bend the knees, and lower both hands to waist level.

4 Move both arms inward across your chest, crossing the wrists, with the left arm closest to your chest. With both palms facing the chest, leave a space between the chest and arms, and under each armpit.

Knee bends slightly

50% 50%

Right foot steps back

50% 50%

合太極 CLOSE T'AI CHI

The steps in the closing sequence of the form are quite similar to those performed at the beginning in *Preparation* (see p. 22), and are designed to relax and stabilize the body as well as to calm the mind. In all the movements, the shoulders are relaxed, with a space left under each armpit, and the head is in alignment with the shoulders, upper body, and waist. The lower back is slightly rounded, and the buttocks are relaxed. The knees are slightly bent, and the lower body should feel heavy and weighted in comparison with the upper body, which should feel light but controlled.

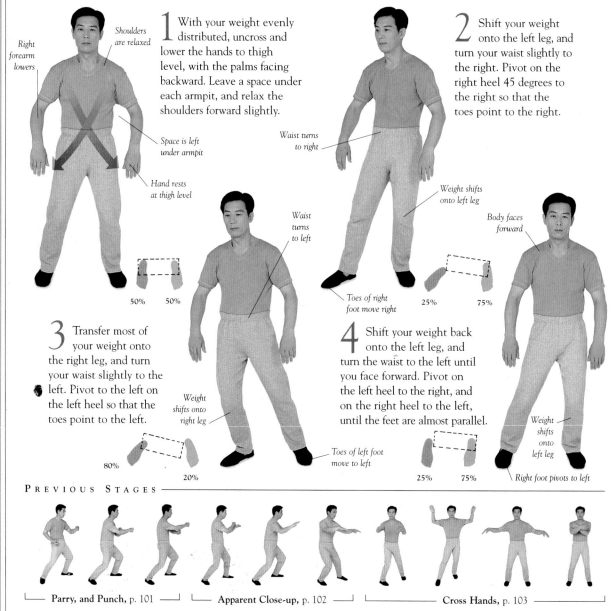

Right forearm lowers

Shoulders are relaxed

1 With your weight evenly distributed, uncross and lower the hands to thigh level, with the palms facing backward. Leave a space under each armpit, and relax the shoulders forward slightly.

Space is left under armpit

Hand rests at thigh level

50%   50%

2 Shift your weight onto the left leg, and turn your waist slightly to the right. Pivot on the right heel 45 degrees to the right so that the toes point to the right.

Waist turns to right

Weight shifts onto left leg

Body faces forward

Waist turns to left

Toes of right foot move right

25%   75%

3 Transfer most of your weight onto the right leg, and turn your waist slightly to the left. Pivot to the left on the left heel so that the toes point to the left.

Weight shifts onto right leg

80%   20%

4 Shift your weight back onto the left leg, and turn the waist to the left until you face forward. Pivot on the left heel to the right, and on the right heel to the left, until the feet are almost parallel.

Toes of left foot move to left

25%   75%

Weight shifts onto left leg

Right foot pivots to left

PREVIOUS STAGES

Parry, and Punch, p. 101 ── ── **Apparent Close-up**, p. 102 ── ── **Cross Hands**, p. 103 ──

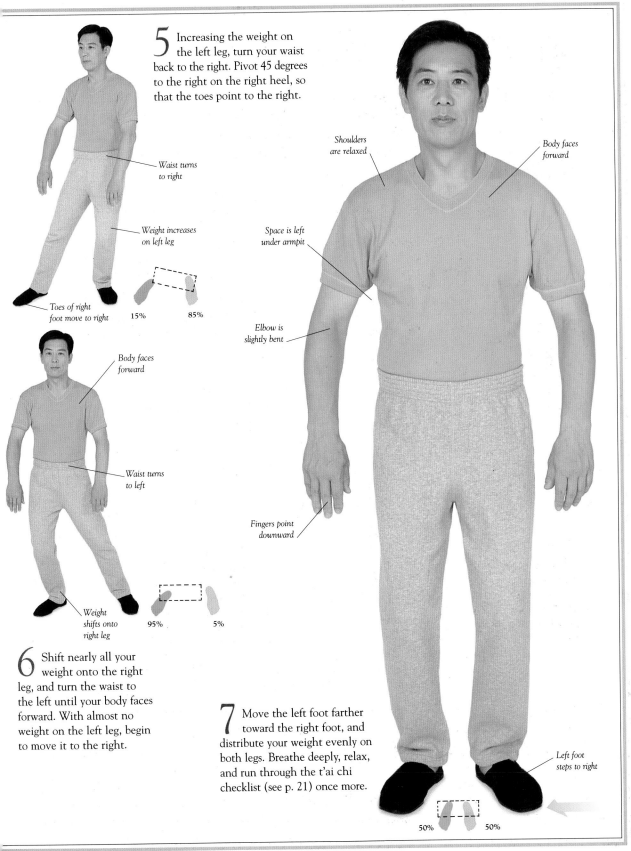

5 Increasing the weight on the left leg, turn your waist back to the right. Pivot 45 degrees to the right on the right heel, so that the toes point to the right.

Waist turns to right

Weight increases on left leg

Toes of right foot move to right

15%   85%

Shoulders are relaxed

Body faces forward

Space is left under armpit

Elbow is slightly bent

Body faces forward

Waist turns to left

Fingers point downward

Weight shifts onto right leg

95%   5%

6 Shift nearly all your weight onto the right leg, and turn the waist to the left until your body faces forward. With almost no weight on the left leg, begin to move it to the right.

7 Move the left foot farther toward the right foot, and distribute your weight evenly on both legs. Breathe deeply, relax, and run through the t'ai chi checklist (see p. 21) once more.

Left foot steps to right

50%   50%

T'AI CHI
SKILLS

Apply your knowledge of the form and begin
to develop your t'ai chi ch'uan with a series of
tests, pushing hands drills, and applications.

DEVELOPING T'AI CHI SKILLS

Once you are familiar with the stances of the form and your rooting skills are developing, you can begin to learn pushing hands drills and applications. The basic stances in the form are improvised upon and adapted in these exercises, which are practiced between partners to heighten anticipatory skills and reflex sensitivity, as well as to develop a sense of mutual cooperation and support.

Left arm is in Left Ward-Off

Left Ward-Off
Like all the stances in the form, Left Ward-Off (see p. 26) is used in pushing hands and applications. The strength of the root in Left Ward-Off can be tested (see below).

Weight is on right leg

TESTING ROOTING SKILLS

Ensuring that the weight is properly distributed down through the body is fundamental to rooting skill; if the weight is wrong, the root will not be stable, and the body will not align correctly. Developing strong rooting skills focuses the mind on the exact position of the body in each stance of the form. As illustrated in the test boxes in the form, an instructor tests weight distribution by applying an even press, push, or pull (see p. 52) to a student's upper body. The strength of pressure is built up as the student's rooting skills slowly increase. When the root is correct, the body stabilizes, and the weight distribution and body alignment fall correctly. This allows for the development of a flexible response to a partner in pushing hands and applications practice; this is the basis of being able to anticipate, and react to, the actions of another person.

Instructor

Instructor pushes against student's left arm

Left arm is in Ward-Off position

Student

Shoulders are relaxed

Body sinks as weight moves down right leg

Buttock muscles are relaxed

Weight is on left leg

Testing the root in *Left Ward-Off*
With the student's left arm in Ward-Off, the instructor applies a double-handed press to her left forearm. The student absorbs this pressure through the left arm, down her body, into the legs, and through the yung ch'uan point (see p. 21) on the left foot, into the ground.

Instructor

Pressure is increased on student's left arm

Student

Weight shifts onto right leg

Right foot is flat on floor

Increasing pressure on the root in *Left Ward-Off*
If the instructor increases the strength of his press against the student's left arm, she relaxes, sinks her body farther, and roots her weight through the right leg, giving her extra stability to absorb the additional pressure of the press. This shifting of weight is a basic move in pushing hands and applications.

PUSHING HANDS DRILLS

The Chinese term for pushing hands is *t'ui shou*, which is usually translated as "pushing," but can also translate as "yielding." In t'ai chi, the normal response to an incoming force is to sink, relax, and yield, since yielding provides the chance to keep in contact with, and monitor, a partner's force, momentum, and balance, which can then be redirected. Pushing hands drills are practiced between partners to develop reflex sensitivity skills and the ability to monitor a partner's intentions from a relaxed physical contact. The drills in this chapter are a sample from an extensive set and involve positions now familiar from the form. For clarity, the partners shown here are called "instructor" and "student."

PUSH HANDS AND SPLIT

In this drill, both partners develop the skills of rooting and turning the waist in *Ward-Off* (see p. 26) to yield and neutralize the force of an incoming *Push* (see p. 29). The whole body moves forward into *Push* – not just the arms and shoulders in isolation – while the leg remains strongly rooted into the ground. The split (see p. 54) in the final stages of this drill brings the instructor's arms up on the inside of the student's arms, halting and deflecting his movement backward.

Instructor

Student

Head is held upright

Arm is in Push *position*

Upper body moves forward in Push *position*

Arm is in Ward-Off position

Lower back is relaxed

Waist turns to right

Knee bends slightly

Right arm forms Ward-Off position

Upper body begins to move forward into Push *position*

Weight shifts onto left leg

Weight is on left leg

1 The instructor forms *Ward-Off* to absorb the student's two-handed *Push*, sinks, and executes *Roll Back*, turning his waist to the right. The student pushes forward from his rooted left leg and turns his waist to the right to test the instructor's yielding skill and waist mobility.

2 The instructor shifts his weight backward onto his left leg, and turns his waist to the right in *Roll Back*, neutralizing the student's *Push*. The student forms *Right Ward-Off*, and the instructor begins to move into *Push*, with his left hand against the student's elbow and his right hand against his wrist.

Weight is on left leg

Right foot is a shoulders' width in front of left foot

Left foot roots at an angle of 45 degrees to right foot

Right arm in Ward-Off position

Waist turns to left

Weight shifts onto right leg

Weight begins to shift onto right leg

Waist turns to right

3 The instructor turns his waist to the left, shifting his weight onto the right foot to provide the momentum for the *Push* against the student's right arm. The student turns his waist to the right and raises his left arm to cover the instructor's right elbow.

4 The student covers the instructor's right elbow with his left hand. In response, the instructor raises his left hand inside the student's right hand, and instead of moving into *Right Ward-Off* (see Step One), begins to move his arms into the split.

Body leans forward slightly

Instructor's arms begin to move into split

Student's hand covers instructor's elbow

Weight is on right leg

Weight is on right leg

Instructor's arms are in split

Weight shifts farther onto right leg

5 As the student's weight shifts onto his right leg, the instructor raises his arms inside the student's arms, splitting them apart by his forward movement so that the student cannot react or strike without a major shift in stance.

Forward movement forces student's arms apart

Left arm overextends

Body moves forward

Weight increases on right leg

Feet stay still throughout drill

6 As the student moves forward, the instructor raises his arms, forcing the student's arms apart, leaving his chest and neck exposed and vulnerable to attack.

SHOULDER ROLL

This drill is a natural progression from *Push Hands and Split* (see p. 108), and helps develop the ability to avoid a threat coming from close quarters, improving splitting skills. The upward splitting motion of the instructor's arms is counteracted in Step Two by his student shrugging and rolling both shoulders backward. This action is based on *Lift Hands* (see p. 32). It requires the student to coordinate the shoulder roll with the instructor's rising arms to protect her exposed throat and neck. In this drill, there is an important connection between being firmly rooted to the ground, being relaxed, and still being flexible enough to anticipate and respond to an attack. It is used as a training exercise, which can be repeated for as long as both partners stay relaxed and coordinated.

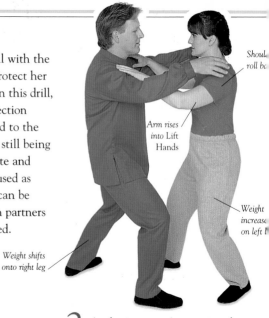

Shou[l]... roll b...

Arm rises into Lift Hands

Weight increase[s] on left [l...]

Weight shifts onto right leg

2 As the instructor's arms rise, the student shifts more weight onto the left leg, moves backward slightly, shrugs, and rolls back her shoulders. Her arms rise into *Lift Hands,* and split the instructor's arms, exposing his throat.

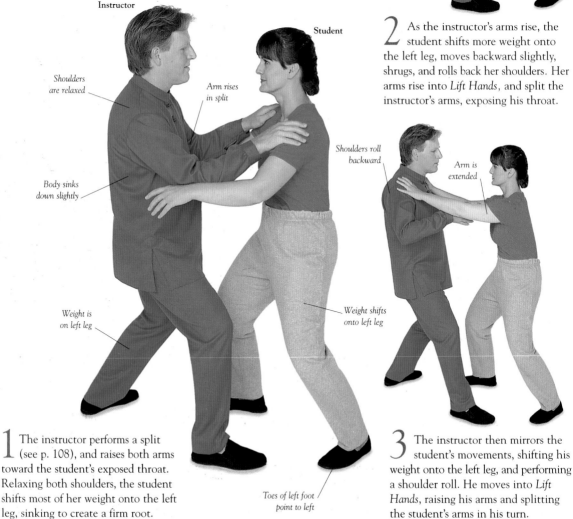

Instructor

Shoulders are relaxed

Arm rises in split

Student

Body sinks down slightly

Shoulders roll backward

Arm is extended

Weight is on left leg

Weight shifts onto left leg

Toes of left foot point to left

1 The instructor performs a split (see p. 108), and raises both arms toward the student's exposed throat. Relaxing both shoulders, the student shifts most of her weight onto the left leg, sinking to create a firm root.

3 The instructor then mirrors the student's movements, shifting his weight onto the left leg, and performing a shoulder roll. He moves into *Lift Hands,* raising his arms and splitting the student's arms in his turn.

PUSHING SHOULDERS AND HIPS

Performed independently, or as a continuation of *Push Hands and Split* (see p. 108), this drill concentrates on keeping the lower back relaxed to maintain a strong root, shifting the root quickly from one leg to another without losing stability, turning the waist, and relaxing the hip joints.

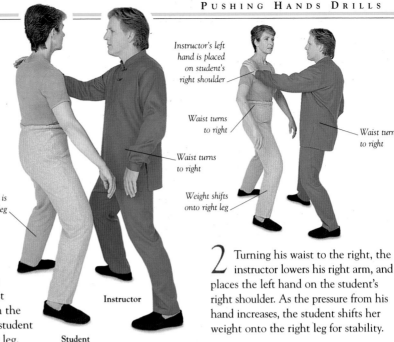

Weight is on left leg

Instructor's left hand is placed on student's right shoulder

Waist turns to right

Waist turns to right

Waist turns to right

Weight shifts onto right leg

Instructor

Student

1 The instructor presses the student's left shoulder with his right hand. In response, the student relaxes, sinks down onto the right leg, and turns her waist to the left. As the pressure from the instructor's hand increases, the student shifts her weight onto the right leg.

2 Turning his waist to the right, the instructor lowers his right arm, and places the left hand on the student's right shoulder. As the pressure from his hand increases, the student shifts her weight onto the right leg for stability.

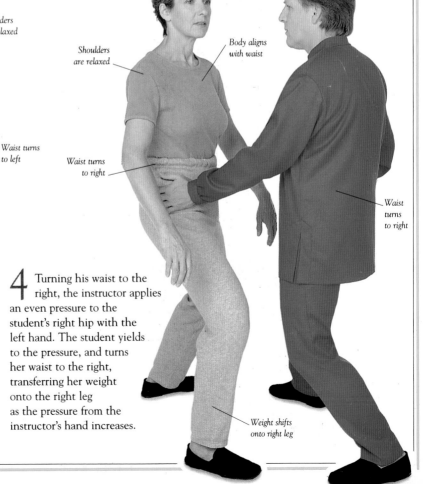

Waist turns to left

Shoulders are relaxed

Shoulders are relaxed

Body aligns with waist

Weight shifts onto left leg

Waist turns to left

Waist turns to right

Waist turns to right

Weight shifts onto right leg

3 Turning his waist to the left, the instructor applies an even pressure to the student's left hip with his left hand. The student yields to the pressure, and turns her waist to the left, transferring her weight onto the left leg as the pressure from the instructor's hand increases.

4 Turning his waist to the right, the instructor applies an even pressure to the student's right hip with the left hand. The student yields to the pressure, and turns her waist to the right, transferring her weight onto the right leg as the pressure from the instructor's hand increases.

ADVANCED PUSH HANDS

In Chinese, this drill is called *si chen shou*, which translates as the "four fixed hands" drill. It incorporates *Ward-Off, Roll Back, Press,* and *Push* (see p. 26) and develops the idea of being relaxed enough to adhere to, or stay in contact with, a partner's movements, to monitor his or her energy. From this so-called "listening energy" (*ting ching*), it is possible to anticipate an attack before it reaches its target, and – with practice – to counter the very strongest of opponents by using the opponent's energy against them. Borrowing a partner's strength in this way is one of the most advanced skills in t'ai chi, and requires persistent practice to learn.

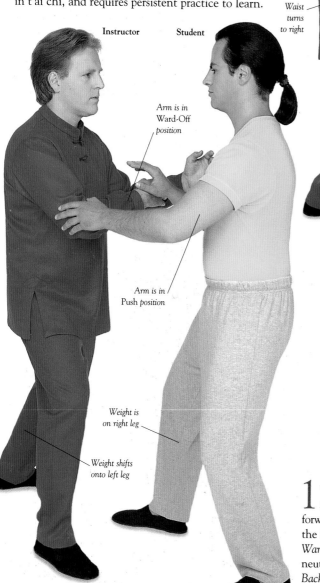

Instructor   Student

Arm is in
Ward-Off
position

Arm is in
Push *position*

Weight is
on right leg

Weight shifts
onto left leg

*Left arm
covers
student's
right elbow*

*Waist
turns
to right*

*Waist
turns
to left*

2 The instructor continues to yield, rolling his waist to the right, while the student turns his waist to the left. As he yields, the instructor brings his left arm into contact with the student's right elbow, preventing it from striking him.

1 With his weight on his right leg, the student moves his upper body forward in a double-handed *Push* against the instructor's right arm, which is in *Ward-Off.* The instructor yields and neutralizes the push by moving into *Roll Back,* shifting his weight onto the left leg.

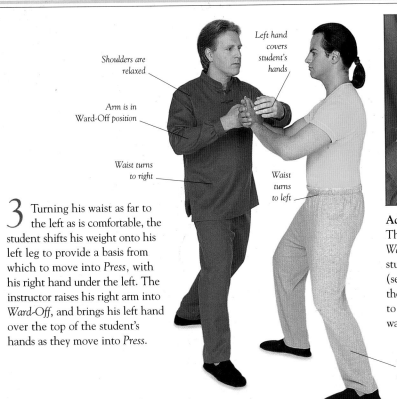

Shoulders are relaxed

Left hand covers student's hands

Arm is in Ward-Off position

Waist turns to right

Waist turns to left

3 Turning his waist as far to the left as is comfortable, the student shifts his weight onto his left leg to provide a basis from which to move into *Press*, with his right hand under the left. The instructor raises his right arm into *Ward-Off*, and brings his left hand over the top of the student's hands as they move into *Press*.

Adhering to the *Press*

The instructor places his right arm into *Ward-Off*, and cups his left hand over the student's hands, which are in a *Press* (see Step Three). The instructor absorbs the force of the *Press* by turning his waist to the right, while the student turns his waist to the left, keeping in light contact.

Weight shifts onto left leg

Arms are in Push position

Left hand moves toward student's left wrist

Waist turns to left

Waist turns to right

4 The student turns his waist to the right to increase the pressure of the *Press*. Turning his waist to the left, the instructor neutralizes the student's *Press* by moving into *Roll Back*. As the student's weight shifts onto the right leg, the instructor turns his waist to the right and slides his left hand to rest over the back of the student's left wrist.

Weight shifts onto right leg

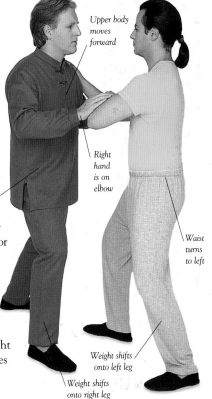

Upper body moves forward

Right hand is on elbow

Waist turns to right

Waist turns to left

5 Turning his waist farther to the right, the instructor places his right hand on the student's left elbow, and shifts his weight onto the right leg, performing a double-handed *Push*. The student lifts his left arm into *Ward-Off*, shifts his weight onto the left leg, and executes *Roll Back*, neutralizing the instructor's *Push*.

Weight shifts onto left leg

Weight shifts onto right leg

APPLICATIONS

These sequences show how the positions, energies, and skills derived from t'ai chi practice are applied in self-defense. The moves in the form are the basis from which to respond to an attack, and are combined with the *ting ching* (see p. 112) taught in pushing hands. There are no set responses, as there are none in genuinely aggressive situations, but it is vital to be stable, relaxed, and flexible in order to anticipate and counter a threat. For clarity, the partners are called "defender" and "opponent," since they are in the applications throughout the form.

APPARENT CLOSE-UP APPLICATION

Based on *Apparent Close-Up* (see p. 40), this application shows how the defender, by relaxing and apparently collapsing his trapped right arm, can retreat and parry with his left arm to turn a vulnerable situation to his advantage, and to stage a counterattack (Step Three).

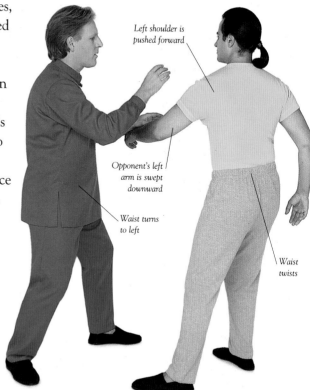

Left shoulder is pushed forward

Opponent's left arm is swept downward

Waist turns to left

Waist twists

2 The defender sweeps the opponent's arms to the right with his left forearm, and keeping a light contact, adheres to it (see p. 112). He pushes the opponent's left arm down to control and unbalance him, leaving the opponent's left side exposed.

Defender tries right-handed punch

Defender
Shoulders are relaxed

Opponent

Right elbow collapses

Waist turns to right

Weight shifts onto right leg

1 The defender parries a right-handed grab with a right-handed punch. The opponent traps the defender's right elbow in his left hand. The defender relaxes, collapses his elbow under the opponent's arm, sinks his weight, and raises his left arm to push the opponent's left arm to the left.

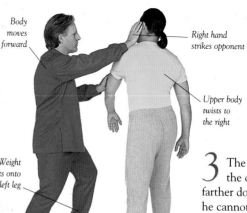

Body moves forward

Right hand strikes opponent

Upper body twists to the right

Weight shifts onto left leg

3 The defender forces the opponent's left arm farther downward so that he cannot retaliate. Shifting his weight onto the left leg, the defender delivers a relaxed palm strike to the left side of the opponent's head.

SHOULDER ROLL APPLICATION

Elements of *Shoulder Roll* (see p. 110), *Lift Hands* (see p. 32), and *Push* (see p. 29) are combined here. This application incorporates the subtle shifting of body weight backward with a relaxed roll-back of the shoulders. When combined with a split (see p. 108), the sequence can be used to stave off an attack to the throat and apply a palm strike to an opponent's chin.

Arms are in Push position

Body is pushed backward slightly

2 With her arms inside the opponent's arms, the defender shifts her weight forward, using momentum powered by *fa ching* energy (see p. 28) to deliver a push to the opponent's chest.

Weight shifts onto right leg

Opponent

Defender

Defender's arms split opponent's arms

Defender's right hand contacts opponent's chin

3 The defender maintains contact with the opponent, simultaneously sliding her left hand along his right arm and her right hand up until it is under his chin. Now in control of him, she turns her waist rapidly to the left, powering the movement of her arms around with her waist to twist him off balance.

Defender's left arm pushes opponent's right arm downward

1 The opponent attempts a double-handed choke hold on the defender's neck. The defender relaxes, shifts her weight back, roots into her left leg, shrugs, and rolls her shoulders backward. With both shoulders and arms relaxed, she raises her arms inside the opponent's forearms and splits them (see p. 108).

Left leg is unbalanced

Waist turns to left

Weight is pushed onto right leg

Weight is on right leg

DIAGONAL FLYING APPLICATION

This sequence combines principles of *Diagonal Flying* (see p. 54) and *Cloud Hands* (see p. 56) in a fluid, dynamic application that shows the importance of creating space, staying relaxed, and rolling the waist. The *Cloud Hands* sequence teaches the ability to sidestep, while rolling the waist in both directions and keeping the arms full of energy. As always in the practice of t'ai chi, the shoulders be relaxed and the arms move with the waist.

Opponent

Defender

Opponent is pushed to right

1 The defender steps to the right and raises his left arm in the *Cloud Hands* position to intercept the opponent's left-handed punch to the chest. On contact, the defender relaxes his stance and turns his waist to the left, turning the opponent to the right, and deflecting the attack.

Left arm rises

Right foot steps to right

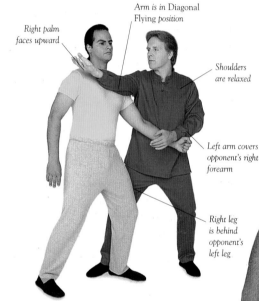

Arm is in Diagonal Flying position

Right palm faces upward

Shoulders are relaxed

Left arm covers opponent's right forearm

Right leg is behind opponent's left leg

2 Turning his waist farther to the left, the defender rests the weight of his relaxed left arm over the opponent's left arm. He brings his right arm across the opponent's throat, the palm facing upward as in *Diagonal Flying*. At the same time, he places his right leg behind the opponent's left leg. (For safety, practice this move with the arm across the chest, not the throat.)

3 The defender turns his waist to the right, forcing the opponent's upper body backward over his right knee. Restraining the opponent's left wrist with his left wrist, the defender has total control of the opponent.

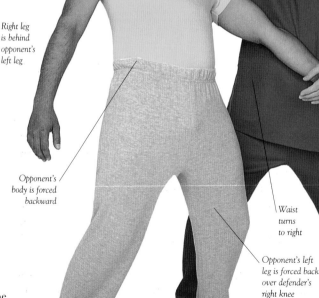

Arm swings to right with waist

Opponent's body is forced backward

Waist turns to right

Opponent's left leg is forced back over defender's right knee

GLOSSARY

The Chinese words that appear in this book have been transliterated using the Wade-Giles system.
For clarity, the glossary gives the Pinyin versions of these Chinese terms in brackets.

Application Adaptations of the moves, energies, and skills learned in the form and pushing hands drills, when applied to self-defense or fighting situations.

Ch'i (*qi*) Vital force or energy flowing through all natural things.

Ching (*jing/jin*) Internal energy (as opposed to muscular strength).

Fa ching (*fa jing*) Springing or forward energy powered by a root connecting the legs to the lower back and upper body.

Form Set pattern of positions and moves fundamental to any martial art.

Kinetic energy Energy stored in the joints and tendons by turning the waist, which is released to increase power.

Press and Push Moves in the form, both requiring the upper body to move forward as a unit. A stable stance is essential, as is a connection between the root, relaxed lower back, and upper body.

Pushing hands *T'ui shou* (*tui shou*) Set drills that develop reflex sensitivity and the ability to root, yield, and monitor a partner's intentions. Competition-level pushing hands have no set drills.

Roll Back Move in the form, creating space in which to maneuver by turning the upper body without moving the feet.

Rooting Lowering gravity and connecting the foot to the ground by relaxing into it, to achieve balance and stability.

Sinking Relaxing the joints and lowering the center of gravity to form a stable connection to the ground. At advanced levels, this is as much mental as physical.

Splitting Taking a force coming from one direction and redirecting it to another.

T'ai chi (*Tai ji*) Translates from Chinese as "great polarity," a concept based on the interdependence of *yin* and *yang*.

T'ai chi ch'uan (*Tai ji quan*) Translates from Chinese as "great polarity boxing." One of China's three "internal" martial arts, teaching a complete understanding of the interplay of *yin* and *yang* forces in mind and body, in order to achieve focusing of internal energy and efficient use of physical power.

Tan t'ien (*dan tian*) Vital point in the abdomen below the navel where the *ch'i* is focused to aid deep, relaxed breathing.

Ting ching (*ting jing*) "Listening energy" or ability to monitor a partner's intention and balance when in physical contact.

Ward-Off Move in the form, using the arm as a barrier or point of contact.

Yielding Relaxing to absorb an incoming force rather than using strength to resist it.

Yin and yang Fundamental qualities in all phenomena that appear to be opposites, but are interdependent. *Yin* qualities are associated with darkness, passivity, water, and the female; *yang* qualities with daylight, activity, air, and the male.

Yung ch'uan (*yong quan*) Vital point at the center of the front part on the sole of each foot, where the balance rests, giving a strong connection to the earth.

CHOOSING A T'AI CHI CLASS

People have different expectations of t'ai chi training; some enjoy it as a series of movements, regarding t'ai chi as a stress-reducing activity, while others regard it as a mind and body discipline or train for health reasons. Some want to develop pushing hands skills and enter competitions. Try to match your particular interest with the emphasis of the class you choose.

Follow some general guidelines before committing to a class. Attend one lesson, and find out as much as you can from fellow students, asking for their views on how the class is taught. Central to your decision to join the class will be the teacher's skill and teaching ability. Beginners will not be able to judge this easily, but they can enquire about a teacher's background – good teachers will be open about who they trained with, knowledgeable about the form they teach, and will include a variety of exercises, pushing hands drills, and applications in their classes. The atmosphere of a class will affect your training progress, so make sure that the class is friendly and cooperative, and that the students support one another during partner work. Avoid classes with an overly competitive edge to the training, and if you are not comfortable, look elsewhere.

In areas outside major cities, there may not be many classes to choose from. In this case, start your t'ai chi training wherever possible, and look around for other options. Training camps and workshops offer intensive courses with qualified teachers. To find out about these, check the listings in martial arts publications, bulletin boards in alternative bookshops, and complementary medicine centers.

INDEX

ACKNOWLEDGMENTS

AUTHOR'S ACKNOWLEDGMENTS

This book is dedicated to the memory of Professor Cheng Man-Ch'ing, Master of the Five Excellences.

I would like to thank Master Tan Ching Ngee of Singapore for his patient teaching and guidance, Tan Mew Hong for her precious advice and beautiful calligraphy, and Nigel Sutton for his knowledge and friendship.

This book could not have been put together without the assistance and skill of the senior instructors and students of the Zhong Ding (Perfect Balance) Traditional Chinese Martial Arts Association. I am particularly indebted to Tom Cahill, Ben Clarke, John Higginson, Vicky Holden, Chris Kaighin, Imelda Maguire, and Damon Townsend.

I am grateful to the following demonstrators for their patience and skill: Vicky Holden, Jenny Parkhill, and Damon Townsend.

PUBLISHER'S ACKNOWLEDGMENTS

Dorling Kindersley would like to thank the following people for their help in the preparation of this book:

Photographer Andy Crawford
Photographer's assistant Gary Ombler
Additional photography Steve Tanner
Demonstrators The publishers would like to extend their special thanks to the main demonstrator, as well as to Vicky Holden, Jenny Parkhill, and Damon Townsend.
Make-up Lynne Maningley, James Miller
Dressmakers Gwen Diamond, Heather Purcell

Illustrators
  Arrows Geoff Denney
  Foot diagrams Jason Little
  Foot artwork Kuo Kang Chen

Editorial assistance Felicity Crowe, Antonia Cunningham, Jude Garlick, Samantha Gray
Design assistance Austin Barlow, Helen Benfield, Sarah Hall, Nicola Webb
Proofreader and indexer Debbi Scholes
Picture research Melissa Albany

PICTURE CREDITS

The publishers are grateful to the following photographers and picture libraries for permission to reproduce their photographs:

Key: t top, **c** centre, **b** bottom, **l** left, **r** right

The Hutchison Library 8**bl**; Mary Evans Picture Library 9**tl**; e. t. Archive 10**bl**; Ken van Sickle and the London School of T'ai Chi Ch'uan and Traditional Health Resources UK Limited 11**tr**.